THE
ORTHODOX
CHURCH

THE ORTHODOX CHURCH

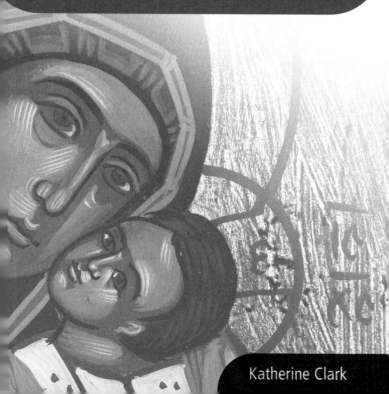

Katherine Clark

·K·U·P·E·R·A·R·D·

Published in Great Britain by
Kuperard, an imprint of Bravo Ltd
59 Hutton Grove, London N12 8DS
www.kuperard.co.uk
Enquiries: office@kuperard.co.uk

Copyright © 2009 Bravo Ltd.

ISBN 978 1 85733 487 6

British Library Cataloguing in Publication Data
A CIP catalogue entry for this book
is available from the British Library

Cover image: Orthodox icon, Rhodes,
Greece. © Rcaucino, Dreamstime.com
Illustrations on pages 23, 67, 110 and 113 by
Panayiotis K. Koumoundouros
The photograhs on pages 13, 45, 82, 115, 116,
121, 125, 129, 141, 145, 149 and 163 are reproduced
by permission of the author.
Photograph on page 107 © Elizabeth Carson
Images on pages 54 Fotolia © inkl, 71 © Jjensen, and
90 © Massimo Finizio

⏵ Contents

List of Illustrations

Christ Pantocrator, "Ruler of all". Sixth-century icon, St Catherine's Monastery, Sinai

⊙ Preface

At the time I first encountered Orthodoxy, I had
had no connection with any religion whatever for
decades. Raised Presbyterian as a child, I was at
first put off by Orthodox practices like kissing
icons, and was shy of the clergy, who appeared so
awesome and so stern. I found almost everything
about Orthodoxy strange, even intimidating – the
ornate surroundings, the unfamiliar objects, the
medieval clerical garb, the highly formal services,
the language, the incense.

But as I grew to know the often tiny, intimate
churches, the non-judgemental, helpful and
insightful clergy, and the Orthodox believers
themselves and their all-pervading relationship
with their religion, I came to love this Church.
Ironically, what particularly attracted me, a
professional 'wordsmith', were its many unspoken,
unwritten 'languages': the symbolism, the artwork,
the ritual, the traditions, the objects with their
special significances, the physical gestures of the
laity and clergy: these expressed things that words
never could. These are the languages of the *logos*,
religious meaning, and I believe they are the truest

medium for worshipping and communicating with God. Especially the icons – at first so cool and remote – came to 'speak' to me.

As for actual language, the words of the Liturgy and other services and the Bible, particularly the Psalms, expressed far better than my own what I wished to say to my Lord; and they instructed me far better than any sermon. As I began to use Orthodox prayers and hymns regularly, they opened up ever profounder meanings to me.

Finally, the Orthodox Church's very antiquity and unchanging practices convinced me of the depth and universality of its message, and of its power as a vehicle for worship. The Church's lack of hierarchy, organisation or even consistency only persuaded me the more. It really is the Holy Spirit, and no human institution, who guides the Orthodox Church and holds it together.

KATHERINE CLARK

⊙ Introduction

This book aims to help Western readers to gain enough insight into the Greek Orthodox Church (and by extension the Eastern Orthodox Church generally) to put them at ease in Orthodox churches, explain what they see, and give them an idea of what is going on there. It assumes that the reader is new to Orthodoxy and may even know little of Christianity generally. Focus is on the essential: what absolutely cannot be left out of any picture of Orthodoxy. The physical church, especially icons, services and common practices are explained, and suggestions are offered to visitors on how to conduct themselves appropriately, so that they are well accepted and feel comfortable.

Several chapters concern the life of Jesus and the beginnings of Christianity. The origins and history of the Church are pursued to the point at which it more or less assumed its present form, with particular attention to its great champion, Constantine the Great. The early centuries of Christianity are stressed because they are largely unfamiliar in the West, and also because Orthodoxy has remained essentially unchanged since then, with the original faith intact.

The book outlines the tenets, nature and holy days of Orthodox belief with the Western reader in mind. The present structure of the Church is described in brief. Finally, the split between the Eastern Church and the Western Church is related and their differences explained in simple terms.

For more detailed information about Orthodoxy and Byzantine history, I especially recommend Metropolitan Kallistos Ware's excellent books, *The Orthodox Church* and *The Orthodox Way*. I also recommend *A History of God*, by Karen Armstrong; *Pagans and Christians*, by Robin Lane Fox; *Byzantium*, by John Julius Norwich; *History of the Byzantine State*, by George Ostrogorsky; *The Byzantine Theocracy*, by Steven Runciman; *The Divine Liturgy Explained*, by Rev. Nicholas M. Elias; *The Holy Sacraments for Orthodox Christians*, by Bishop Valerian D. Trifa; and, in German, *Konstantin der Grosse und seine Zeit*, by Manfred Clauss; *Die Kirchenväter und ihre Zeit*, by Hartmut Leppin; *Byzanz*, by Ralph-Johannes Lilie; *Kunst und Liturgie der Ostkirche in Stichworten unter Berücksichtigung der Alten Kirche*, by Konrad Onasch; and *Geschichte des Frühen Christentums*, by Friedhelm Winkelmann. These, along with my personal experience, are the sources of the information here.

Old Testament quotations are from the Septuagint, the English translation by Sir Lancelot Charles Lee Brenton (first published in 1844). New Testament quotations are from the King James version of the Bible.

My warmest thanks for well-informed and active assistance to those fine writers and good friends Willard Manus and Jeffrey Carson, to Pfarrer Gerd Stauch, to my siblings in the faith Anastasia and Steven Charters, and, as in all I do, to my husband and mentor James A. Clark, *sine qua non.*

Ἐν ἀγάπη καὶ εὐγνωμοσύνη εἰς
τὸν Πρωτ. Πέτρον Χερουβείμ
τὴν Πρεσ. Εἰρήνη Χερουβείμ
τὸν Μοναχὸν Ἰάκωβον Γουΐλλιαμς

Ἡ παιδεία Κυρίου ἀνοίγει μου τὰ ὦτα,
ἐγὼ δὲ οὐκ ἀπειθῶ οὐδὲ ἀντιλέγω.

Ἡσαΐας Ν:ε

The instruction of the Lord God
opens my ears, and I do not disobey,
nor do I dispute.

Isaiah 50: 5

⊙ *The Mother of God the Most Holy Theotokos and Ever-Virgin Mary. Contemporary Greek icon*

Chapter 1

Jesus' Life

The life of Jesus Christ and the events that immediately
preceded and followed it are at the root of all Christian
worship. Thus our account of the Eastern Orthodox
Church is best begun with the Christian 'story'.

What we know of Jesus' life comes from the Gospels
(from "godspel" in Old English: the 'good news') of SS
Matthew, Mark, Luke and John in the New Testament
of the Bible. These texts were written between about
AD 60 and 80 – that is, about thirty to fifty years after
Jesus died. He was born to a Jewish family in
Bethlehem in Judea, just southwest of Jerusalem,
during the reign of the Roman Emperor Augustus,
nominally in the first year of our era. Since our era
begins with Christ's birth, dates are preceded by AD, in
Latin *anno domini*, 'in the year of our Lord', or followed
by BC for 'before Christ'. Much of what is now Israel and
the Palestinian Territories was then a kingdom within
the Roman Empire, occupied by Roman forces and
under the supervision of a Roman governor. At the time
of Jesus' birth, the king of Judea was Herod the Great.

Jesus' parents were from Nazareth in what is now
northern Israel. His earthly father, Joseph, was a
carpenter, a widower who already had children by his

first wife. But in fact Jesus had no earthly father: his young mother, Mary, though promised to Joseph, was still a virgin: she conceived her child miraculously, through the Holy Spirit, upon the visit to her of the Archangel Gabriel. This event, the Annunciation, is celebrated each year on 25 March. In religious art, one sees the winged Angel Gabriel addressing the Virgin, robed in blue, a dove representing the Holy Spirit hovering between them, as often depicted on the holy gates at the centre of the iconostasis (see Chapter 7: Visiting an Orthodox Church).

⊙ *Byzantine icon of the Archangel Gabriel, c.1387–95*

Jesus was born nine months later, on 25 December, in Bethlehem, where his father had taken the family for tax registration purposes. Although the Gospels tell us that the birth took place in a stable, the inn in Bethlehem being full, Orthodox art shows the nativity in a cave, in accord with the events related in the Protoevangelium of James, a non-canonical early Christian account. Three wise men or kings from the East, guided by a star, came to adore the infant Jesus, as did shepherds, to whom an angel had appeared in their fields, announcing the miraculous birth, accompanied by a 'multitude of the heavenly host' singing 'Glory to God in the highest, and on earth peace, good will toward men'. We celebrate the birth of Jesus Christ with the holiday that bears his name: Christmas (Christ's mass).

His parents presented him at the Temple forty days later, on 2 February. This scene, too, is popular in Orthodox iconography: the mother presenting the baby to the aged priest Simeon, to whom God had promised that he would see the world's salvation before he died. Simeon, beholding the child, expressed his joy in the beautiful words that are repeated every evening at the vesper service: 'Lord, now lettest thou thy servant depart in peace, according to thy word: For mine eyes have seen thy salvation, which thou hast prepared before the face of all people; a light to lighten the Gentiles, and the glory of thy people Israel.' (Luke 2: 29–32.) To this

day Orthodox mothers present their babies to the
priest at their church forty days after giving birth.

We then lose sight of Jesus until he is about
twelve years of age, when he appears in the
Temple in Jerusalem, disputing on equal terms
with the learned scholars there. After that he drops
out of sight again until he is about thirty, when he
is baptised in the Jordan river by his cousin John, a
popular preacher and hermit living in desert places.
John foresaw Jesus' coming, saying to the people
who came to hear him preach, 'I indeed baptize you
with water, but one mightier than I cometh, the
latchet of whose shoes I am not worthy to unloose:
he shall baptize you with the Holy Ghost.' And
indeed, when Jesus presents Himself for baptism,
John recognises his divinity and says, 'Behold the
lamb of God, which taketh away the sin of the
world.' And 'the heaven was opened, and the Holy
Spirit descended in a bodily shape like a dove upon
him, and a voice came from heaven, which said,
Thou art my beloved Son, in thee I am well
pleased.' The feast of Theophany (Epiphany in the
West) on 6 January celebrates this event. On this
occasion the waters are blessed, and in some
countries – in Greece, for instance – intrepid local
youth dive into the freezing waters to retrieve the
cross the priest tosses into them.

Jesus gathered about himself twelve disciples:
Peter and his brother Andrew, James and his
brother John, Philip, Bartholomew, Thomas,

Matthew, another James, Thaddeus, Simon the
Zealot and Judas Iscariot. A number of women also
gathered around him and are mentioned by name:
Mary and Martha, sisters, Johanna, Susanna, Mary
Magdalene and many others.

Jesus travelled with his disciples from place to
place in Israel and Judea, preaching to the people
who assembled to hear him. His message can be
easily summarised: people should love, first, God,
their creator, with all their hearts and all their
minds and all their strength, and they should love
other people as they love their own selves. He
taught them how to pray with a clear and simple
prayer, known today as the Lord's Prayer, which is
spoken in every Orthodox service:

*Our Father who art in heaven, hallowed be thy
name. Thy kingdom come, thy will be done on
earth as it is in heaven. Give us this day our
daily bread, and forgive us our debts as we
forgive our debtors. And lead us not into
temptation but deliver us from evil.*

He announced a new set of human priorities and
principles that expressed God's sympathy with the
poor and downtrodden, as revolutionary an idea
then as it is now. These 'Beatitudes' or 'blessings'
gave a promise of hope to the impoverished and the
suffering in a world that did even less to succour
them than ours does today. He said:

Blessed are the poor in spirit: for theirs is the kingdom of heaven.

Blessed are they that mourn: for they shall be comforted.

Blessed are the meek: for they shall inherit the earth.

Blessed are they which do hunger and thirst after righteousness: for they shall be filled.

Blessed are the merciful: for they shall obtain mercy.

Blessed are the pure in heart: for they shall see God.

Blessed are the peacemakers: for they shall be called the children of God.

Blessed are they which are persecuted for righteousness sake: for theirs is the kingdom of heaven.

Blessed are ye when people shall revile you and persecute you and say all manner of evil against you falsely for my sake.

Rejoice, and be exceeding glad: for great is your reward in heaven.

(Matthew 5: 3–12)

Although Jesus addressed particularly the lower levels of society – the poor, thieves, tax extortionists, prostitutes, etc. – his message appealed to people of all kinds, including the rich and even Roman military officers. His method of teaching often involved parables – little stories with a moral point – which stayed in people's minds and gave them food for thought. The parables of the prodigal son, the wise and foolish virgins with their lamps, the servants and their talents, the house built on sand, the seed falling on fertile or stony ground are some of the ones that are best known.

Jesus also performed many miracles, such as multiplying a few fish and loaves of bread into enough food to feed a huge assembly of people, changing water into wine, walking upon the sea and calming it, driving out of people the demons that possessed them, healing people of leprosy, blindness, menstrual disorders and madness, and even raising the dead. These miracles attested to Jesus' being in truth a man filled with divine power: the son of God – though as he said again and again, it was the people's faith that healed them. And in a great mystical event, celebrated on 6 August as the Transfiguration, He appeared on Mount Tabor near Nazareth in what is now Israel to Peter, James and John, radiant in the light of His glory, the Son of God indeed.

Jesus' activities did not only win him friends, however. As his popularity grew, he was sometimes called 'King of the Jews', a title that did not sit well with the occupying Roman power or with the Jewish establishment, which sought to cooperate with the Romans, preserve Jewish tradition and law, and keep the peace in their occupied country. As matters came to a head, Jesus foresaw what was coming and held a final dinner in Jerusalem with his disciples on the eve of the great Jewish feast of Passover in about the year 33 of our era. This 'last supper' with his twelve disciples is often depicted in art. It was at that dinner that he broke bread and passed pieces to his disciples, saying as he did so that the bread was to be seen as his body, broken on their behalf. He also passed wine to them saying that the wine was his blood. He asked them when they ate bread and drank wine in future to do this in remembrance of him. And Christians do just this every time they participate in the sacrament of communion.

That same evening he went with them to pray in the garden of Gethsemane just outside the walls of Jerusalem, and it was there that Judas Iscariot, one of the twelve, betrayed him – ironically identifying him with a kiss to the multitude from the Temple authorities who were searching for him. He was ultimately brought before the Roman governor at the time, Pontius Pilate, who yielded to the pressure of the mob roused by the Jewish leaders, convicted Jesus of sedition, and condemned him to death by crucifixion, a common but particularly cruel, lingering and humiliating form of execution reserved for outlaws and the lowest ranks of society.

Jesus was crucified at about 9.00 in the morning on a Friday, declared dead and removed from the

cross at about 3.00 the same afternoon, and given
to friends for immediate burial. The Orthodox
remember Christ's suffering and crucifixion
throughout Great Week, the week before Easter
Sunday, and particularly on Great (Good) Friday, the
day of Jesus' crucifixion. His mother, disciples and
friends, bereft of their beloved leader, were grieved
and desperate. They loved him personally, but even
more important, he was their rabbi, their teacher –
the fount of all their hopes in this world and the
next. They had built their lives and futures around
him, and they counted on him and the promises he
had made to them for eternal life.

On the following Sunday morning – that is, the
third day – some of his women followers visited his
tomb, where they found to their horror and
astonishment that it was wide open and empty.
They supposed that the tomb had been desecrated
and the body stolen by the Jewish establishment or
the Romans, who for their part, would surely
believe Jesus' followers had stolen it to stage a
miracle. As Mary Magdalene turned aside and
wept, Jesus himself appeared to her and called her
by name: He had risen from the dead! Like all
Christians, the Orthodox celebrate this great
miracle at Easter, the foremost festival in the
Orthodox Church calendar. The women told the
astonished disciples the amazing news, and that
same day Jesus appeared to them as they met

together, huddled behind closed doors for fear of the wrath of the authorities.

During the ensuing weeks, Jesus appeared on various occasions to a number of persons, speaking and even dining with them and showing the wounds from his crucifixion to St Thomas, who would not believe the miracle until he saw them (thus 'doubting Thomas').

On the fortieth day after His resurrection, Jesus was taken up bodily into heaven. This we celebrate as Ascension Day, forty days after Easter. Again his followers were left alone and desolate – but only for ten days this time. Fifty days after Jesus rose from the dead, the Comforter or Counsellor He had promised to send to abide with them for ever – the Holy Spirit – descended upon them all, conferring on these simple, uneducated persons great faith and powers: eloquence, charisma and the ability to speak foreign languages. And thus the Holy Orthodox Church was founded, imbued with the Holy Spirit, on Pentecost, fifty days after Easter.

Chapter 2

The Early Church

In AD 33, after Jesus had lived his life, preached his message, performed his miracles, died, risen from the dead and ascended into heaven, Christianity was still a long way from being an organised 'Church' as we understand the term. How, then, did Christianity actually get started as an institution? Just what happened to the Christians – Jesus' friends, those who had heard him preach, those who heard the new doctrine from others, and all of the generations of Christians that followed them – over the next two hundred and eighty years until Christianity was finally legitimised in AD 313?

We do not know very precisely. The new religion appealed largely to a small minority of the population of the Roman Empire – a predominantly poor, uneducated and powerless minority at that. Whenever Christianity did show signs of rising to greater prominence, it attracted the attention of the authorities, who viewed it as theologically, philosophically, socially and politically suspect and a threat to the status quo. They reacted by firmly and repeatedly quashing it. So Christians kept a very low profile, meeting in secret in people's

⊙ *Early Christian painting of Jesus flanked by his disciples, from the catacomb of Domitilla, Rome*

houses, in out-of-the-way places in the countryside, or underground in catacombs.

What we do know about the first centuries of Christianity is mostly to be found in the New Testament of the Bible, written between AD 50 and 120, the writings of the Apostolic Fathers (the second- and third-generation Christians of the first century and the first half of the second century) and, ironically, through records of the verbal and physical attacks on Christians and Christianity by their detractors. Traces of early Christianity are also to be found in a few catacombs with early Christian art and artefacts – fortunately and wonderfully preserved down through the millennia – where Christians met and worshipped in secret and buried their dead. The most famous and extensive of these are in Rome, but they are also to be found in much more unlikely places, such as the Greek island of Milos.

The Beginnings

The Eastern Orthodox Church traces its founding to Pentecost, fifty days after Jesus' resurrection. On this occasion, as we read in the Bible in the Acts of the Apostles, Jesus' eleven surviving disciples and Matthias – chosen to replace Judas, Jesus' betrayer (who had hanged himself) – had gathered together in Jerusalem. As Jesus had promised, the Holy Ghost or Holy Spirit – the Comforter and Spirit of Truth, the well-spring and source of spiritual life, Who is present everywhere and in all things – descended upon them. As we read in Acts 2: 1–4:

'And when the day of Pentecost was fully come, they were all with one accord in one place. And suddenly there came a sound from heaven as of

a rushing mighty wind, and it filled all the house where they were sitting. And there appeared unto them cloven tongues like as of fire, and it sat upon each of them. And they were all filled with the Holy Ghost, and began to speak with other tongues, as the Spirit gave them utterance.'

The visitation of the Holy Spirit to this assembly transformed them from a collection of individual followers of Christ to a body of worshippers with a shared object: in Greek an *ecclesia* or assembly of persons 'summoned forth' – in other words, a Church. Word of these wonders quickly spread, ' . . . and the same day there were added unto them about three thousand souls' (Acts 2: 41). The Christian Church was on its way.

This principle of interaction between the Holy Spirit and an *assembly* of Christians has defined the decision-making structure of the Eastern Orthodox Church throughout history right down to our own time two thousand years later. It distinguishes the Orthodox Church significantly in both theory and practice from the hierarchically organised Roman Catholic Church. The Eastern Church is entirely decentralised, with no central authority at its head. Its tenets and operations are still determined – as at Pentecost – not by any single individual but by assemblies of Christians under the guidance of the Holy Spirit.

The Influence of Greek

The three thousand souls who joined the infant Church at Pentecost were for the most part Jews, primarily poor and simple people like most of Jesus' followers. However, many were 'Hellenised' Jews: Greek-speakers who had adopted the Greek culture that predominated at that time among educated urban citizens of the Roman Empire of whatever nationality, much as the English language and American culture tend to predominate in our world today. Stephen, the first Christian martyr, was one such Hellenised Jew. In the early third century BC, the Egyptian king, Ptolemy II Philadelphus, had commissioned the translation of the Old Testament from Hebrew into Greek for his library in Alexandria. This translation, called the Septuagint after the committee of seventy scholars who completed it, was welcomed by Hellenised Jews who had lost their command of Hebrew. Thus it came to be used among early Christians and by the Orthodox Church. Altogether, language was to play a very important role in Christian Church history and in the evolution of the Orthodox Church: the power conferred by the Holy Spirit to those assembled at Pentecost to 'speak with tongues' – that is, to be fluent in a variety of languages – was thus of quite special significance.

Greek was the lingua franca not only of Hellenised Jews but of intellectuals throughout the

Roman Empire, who read Aeschylus, Sophocles, Euripides, Plato and Aristotle in the original Greek. It remained the dominant language of Athens and Alexandria, whose universities and libraries (400,000 volumes in Alexandria!) made them, together with Rome, the intellectual capitals of the day.

Greek was also spoken by cultivated Romans, travellers, merchants and many other people throughout the Roman Empire. Jesus and his closest followers spoke Aramaic, a Semitic language related to both Hebrew and Arabic that was spoken throughout the Near East for some twelve hundred years, from about the Babylonian Exile (586–538 BC) until after the rise of Islam (AD 620). We do not know how many of them knew some Greek, too. In any case, it was very fortunate for the success of Christianity that the books of the New Testament did not appear in Aramaic but in Greek, specifically in *koine* ('the common [tongue]'), which even Greeks today can understand with a little effort. Anything written in Greek was assured of reaching a wide audience. It was the Greek language that put Christianity on the map internationally right from its inception.

The Roman Empire and the Latin Language

Aside from Greek, many people even in the eastern part of the Roman Empire knew – in addition to their own national language or dialect – some Latin, the

language of the occupying Roman administration
and military forces. Only people living in rural areas
would have been confined to a local language or
dialect alone. The people living in or visiting
Jerusalem came from all over the Roman Empire:
the city was every bit as international when Jesus
lived there as it is today.

With a unified and effective administration, two
international languages, a strong army, a good
network of roads, relative security for travel by land
and sea (that is, some safety from pirates and
marauders), and toleration of every sort of idea and
practice except rebellion against the state, the
Roman Empire thus offered very favourable
conditions for the spread of not only trade but
knowledge, ideas and customs from one end of the
civilised world to the other – from Egypt to the
British Isles, from Spain to Persia. Indeed, the upper
classes, wherever they might live within the Roman
Empire, often shared similar religious, social and
cultural practices.

The Roman Empire also offered freedom of
worship to every kind of religion, cult and sect,
from the Asian earth goddess Cybele in the East to
the Druids of Britain in the West, from Osiris, the
Egyptian god of the dead, to the Scythian gods
north of the Black Sea. The only religious duty the
state required of all of its citizens was that they
respect and serve the *salus publica* – the common
weal or public good of the Roman Empire itself –

and that they worship the Roman emperor as a god. Otherwise, they were free to worship, additionally, any deity or deities in virtually any way they chose.

The Jews

In this divine pot-pourri, the Jews stood out with their one god and their contempt for the empire's polytheistic practices; their more spiritually sophisticated concept of monotheism gained in popularity as polytheism lost its appeal. Especially after the Romans destroyed the Temple in Jerusalem in AD 70, Jews spread from one end of the Roman Empire to the other, establishing synagogues where they could assemble and worship. They remained unified by their Law – codified in the Old Testament of the Bible and continually debated and refined with commentaries – their widespread literacy, their very ancient tradition and their national language, so that they could spread out over great distances without losing their identity. These far-flung communities contributed materially to Jewish trade and prosperity, as Jews could travel anywhere throughout the vast expanses of the Roman Empire and count on being taken in, housed and fed, informed about local trade, social and religious practices, and assisted with business or personal connections.

Because of its great antiquity, Judaism was tolerated by the Roman authorities – despite the refusal of Jews to submit to the pagan practices required of other inhabitants of the empire, such as worshipping the emperor or other state deities. All of these advantages of Judaism directly served Christianity in its early years, because, at least until AD 70, Christianity was universally viewed – by Jews, pagans, and Christians alike – as fundamentally a Jewish sect. The Jewish network of supportive, sympathetic and like-minded people markedly smoothed the way for the spread of Christianity during the first century AD.

Thus from AD 33 until the 60s and later, Jesus' disciples and adherents of his message spread Christianity throughout the cities of the Roman Empire, often heading from one synagogue to the next, where they could hope to be well received and heeded. The key figure among champions of Jesus' teachings was certainly St Paul, but there were hundreds of other, unknown but comparably zealous believers – many of whom had themselves known Jesus personally or had heard him preach. Tradition has it that Jesus' disciples fanned out throughout the Roman Empire and beyond: St Thomas to India, St Matthew to Syria, St Simon the Zealot to Persia, St Bartholomew to Kazakhstan, St Andreas to southern Russia, St Philip to Phrygia, St John to Ephesus, St James the brother of St John to Spain, St Peter to Rome, St Mark to Egypt and finally St Paul around the Aegean Sea and then to Rome. St James, Jesus' step-brother, remained in

Jerusalem. This period came to an end between AD 62 and 70 with the deaths and martyrdoms of many of this first generation of Christians, most notably SS Peter, James and Paul.

As time went by, too, Jewish Christians distanced themselves increasingly from the Jewish law of the Torah and Talmud – though essentially retaining the Jewish moral code – and developed practices of their own. St Paul in his epistles in the New Testament repeatedly stresses the importance of the spirit as opposed to the letter of the law. Besides, Jewish Christians were being joined by ever-larger numbers of 'Gentiles' – non-Jews – who soon predominated. As early as AD 49, non-Jewish adherents of the new religion were present in significant enough numbers to spark debate among the Apostles about whether converts should be obliged to observe Jewish dietary and other laws, such as circumcision, or not. A first council of Christians was held at that time in Jerusalem to debate just this issue, as related in the book of Acts in the New Testament, and the landmark decision was taken that Gentiles could become Christians without being circumcised or adopting Jewish dietary practices. As St Peter pointed out, since even Jews could not keep the law, Gentile Christians should not be expected to. This decision was pivotal in opening the new sect to people of every nation and background and in distinguishing it from Judaism.

The Christians divided clearly and decisively from the Jews in AD 70, when Jewish Christians refused to join in the Jewish revolt against the Romans that culminated in the destruction of the ancient Temple in Jerusalem, before whose wall Jews pray to this day. Jesus had said, 'My kingdom is not of this world', so early Christians assiduously avoided taking sides in temporal quarrels, including the revolt. Traditional Jews viewed their lack of commitment as disloyalty, however, and ceased to count Christians among their numbers.

Revolutionary Ideas

What attracted people to Christianity in the first century of our era? For many people living in the Roman Empire at that time, Christianity offered a sort of 'solution'. Where philosophy primarily raised questions, Christianity offered answers: it rejected the sensual excesses – offensive to some – of many other religions; it presented a life of the spirit to intellectuals unfulfilled by the life of the mind; it had a firm and comprehensible moral code favouring stability and family life; its monotheism appeared more plausible than polytheism to the spiritually sophisticated; it gave direction to people looking for a 'right' way to live; it imbued suffering with meaning and offered hope to the desperate; it comforted the downtrodden and miserable with the promise of eternal life; it treated its members as equals, without regard to wealth, social rank or gender; it increased the stature of simply being human through its tenet that God himself had taken human form; it reassured the anxious in times when fierce barbarian tribes were beginning to shake the foundations of the Roman Empire; and it promised eventual vindication for the suffering of abuse and injustice, punishment of the wicked, and a final reward to the legions of the meek and humble. In practical terms, Christian communities provided widows, orphans and other vulnerable groups with some degree of social security – food, shelter and protection – in this world, where they were otherwise often without any other recourse.

We can hardly imagine today how utterly revolutionary many of these ideas were at a time when a multitude of gods and religions was part of everyday life, when the most advanced medical opinion of the day declared women to be biologically inferior to men, when slavery was universally accepted and viewed as an economic necessity, and when savage forms of punishment such as crucifixion were the rule.

Christianity afflicted the comfortable and comforted the afflicted: its appeal was universal. But most revolutionary of all, it substituted for law – both the Jewish law of the Old Testament and secular Roman law – a transcendent and novel foundation for human behaviour and morality:

love. Jesus' new commandment – that people were to love God and other people – made love, of all things, the determinant and measure of all behaviour and morality. Surely this idea is as revolutionary today as it was then!

Christian writings – letters, accounts, documents, sermons, dialogues, tales of martyrdoms, etc. – were steadily collected and codified, and unacceptable texts separated from what was acceptable in Christian terms. Though the dates are constantly being revised, scholars agree that the first Christian texts – the letters of St Paul – were probably written from *c.* AD 50, some seventeen years after Christ's crucifixion, until St Paul's death in about AD 64. It has been claimed that the Gospel of St John was written during this early period as well, though traditional scholarship has placed it later.

The Gospel according to St Mark was probably written around AD 70; the Gospels of SS Matthew and Luke about AD 80, the Acts of the Apostles around AD 90 and the Revelation around AD 92/93. The Apostolic Fathers Clement, Ignatius and Polycarp wrote their letters and treatises between about AD 95 and 110. One of the key writings of this very early Christian period, the Didache, which outlines the early Christian sacraments of baptism and communion, was also written at about this same time.

Organisation in the Young Church

From the year AD 70 to roughly the end of the first century, Christianity underwent a period of geographical expansion and institutional consolidation. Christian flocks needed organisation and leadership, and within a few decades of Jesus' death the three clerical offices were established that still obtain in Orthodoxy today: bishop, presbyter (priest) and deacon. The bishop was then, as today, the spiritual leader of Christians in a given geographical area. Bishops led the prayer meetings and 'love feasts', where Christians shared wine and bread, that soon evolved into formal Church services. They counselled Christians in their community on correct behaviour in regard to religious practice, property and family life, and saw that widows, orphans, the poor and the sick were cared for, often taking them right into their own homes. As the numbers of Christians grew and bishops could no longer cope with their many responsibilities, they began to appoint priests to represent them: to conduct services and administer the sacraments on their behalf. Both bishops and presbyters eventually came to be assisted during services and otherwise by deacons.

By the end of the first century the first sacraments – baptism and communion – had been established in Church practice, and rules for conducting them set out. A basic moral code for Christians took form and became distinct from that of other religions and philosophies. The earliest Christian writers – the four evangelists SS Matthew, Mark, Luke and John, St Paul, and the Apostolic Fathers, who wrote at about the same period or shortly after – were at pains to articulate just how Christians were and were not to behave. St Paul, in particular, tirelessly endeavours in his letters to the early Christian communities to clarify the Christian view of faith, marriage, divorce, circumcision, diet, the state, and more.

Still, during the first and second centuries of our era, Christians were entirely insignificant within the larger picture of the Roman Empire as a whole. The writings and activities of the Christians were of little general interest and were simply unknown or ignored as peripheral. The Roman Empire was full of sects.

The Persecutions

Although Christians, starting with St Paul, preached loyalty to the secular power and submission to state authority, Christianity's very novelty made it suspect. The Roman state was itself venerable and conservative – more comfortable with long-established and traditional religions. Christianity was novel, vigorous and uncompromising. Christians owed their allegiance first to Christ and their own consciences and only secondarily to the emperor and state. Despite their basic acceptance of the temporal power, they refused to acknowledge the emperor's divinity or to sacrifice to state gods such as 'Victoria', so that whatever the facts, their loyalty to the state appeared uncertain. The Christians were not revolutionaries in a political sense. Their kingdom was not of this world, as Jesus had said. But unlike the other religions of the empire (except the Jews), the Christians were both monotheistic and 'exclusive': that is, they claimed that their religion was not only *a* road but *the* road to divine favour, salvation and eternal life. This position did not endear them to the more easy-going, often wealthy and powerful adherents of other, laxer religions.

As Christians increased in numbers and influence, the state came to view them first as an irritation in the body politic and finally as a threat to the status quo. At that point it began to crack down on them. The first persecution erupted as early as AD 64, when, under the Emperor Nero, Christians were blamed for the burning of Rome, and further persecutions soon spread throughout the empire. As Christianity attracted the attention of the intellectual establishment, pagan philosophers, scholars and theologians began to criticise it, lending the state repression moral and social legitimacy. Paradoxically, the steadily increasing severity and

scope of the persecutions attested to the new
religion's growing success.

Depending on the disposition and confidence
of the reigning emperor, the persecutions continued
off and on for some two hundred and fifty years,
from 64 until 311, the pace quickening as

⊙ *The martyrdom in Rome (c. AD 107) of St Ignatius, third bishop
and patriarch of Antioch, also known as Theophorus, for he 'bore
Christ within his breast'.*

Christianity grew. In the year 248, the city of Rome celebrated its thousandth birthday with lavish pagan celebrations; in 249 the emperor declared that all inhabitants of the empire were required to sacrifice to the state gods. The Christians, of course, refused, and in 250–1 were persecuted throughout the empire as a result. Another great wave of persecution swept the empire in 257–8. Many smaller or local persecutions followed.

But the final and most horrible persecutions took place over a period of eight years, from 303–11, under the Emperor Diocletian: these nearly eliminated the infant Church entirely. As the lives of the martyrs tell us, and Christian art has made immediate in gruesome detail for over seventeen hundred years, human ingenuity knew no bounds when it came to stamping out the perfidious new sect. People were not only imprisoned, dispossessed or exiled for their belief – which at that time meant inevitable poverty and often death – but crucified (both right-side up and upside down), burned on the cross, grilled over fires, hacked to bits, stretched on wheels, pulled apart by teams of horses, bound tight and shot full of arrows, fed to wild animals, beheaded, flayed, dressed in animal skins and hunted by dogs, stoned, and so on.

Some Christians actually welcomed martyrdom for the immediate salvation it promised and eternal life in paradise. Still, such horrors led most to keep their beliefs to themselves. They worshipped in private houses and buried their dead in catacombs beneath city streets or in caves in the countryside. They used secret signs and symbols to identify themselves, such as the monogram XP (for Christ in Greek) and the pictogram of a fish, in Greek ΙΧΘΥΣ (EEKH-thees), the letters of which stand for ΙΗΣΟΥΣ (Jesus), ΧΡΙΣΤΟΣ (Christ), ΘΕΟΥ (God's), ΥΙΟΣ (Son), ΣΩΤΗΡ (Saviour). A burial inscription dated 190 and significantly written in a kind of code attests to how far Christianity had spread geographically: 'I saw Syria's plains and all cities as far as Nisibis. I crossed the Euphrates and found fellow-believers everywhere . . . And with faith I dined everywhere on the great and pure fish [Christ], straight from the spring [Godhead], caught by a pure virgin [Mary, mother of Jesus] and served with the wine [Christ's blood/Eucharist wine] belonging with it – mixed wine [wine/blood and water] – and bread [Christ's body].'

So for nearly three hundred years – from 33 to 311 – Christianity was practised in secret or semi-secret, and our knowledge of these years is correspondingly sketchy and intermittent. Yet its very secrecy no doubt lent Christianity a special attraction, and it spread throughout society (primarily urban society) from slaves to aristocrats, all over the Roman Empire and beyond it to the Persians, Armenians, Georgians, Ethiopians, Sudanese, Indians, Arabs, Asians, Germans and

Slavs. Armenia was the first country to adopt
Christianity as its state religion, in AD 301.

Divisions within the Early Church

Right from the start there were disagreements
among Christians about proper Christian behaviour,
policy, practices, jurisdiction and dogma, some of
them recorded in the New Testament in the Acts of
the Apostles and in the letters of St Paul, others in
correspondence. Who was in charge? Could
someone who had reneged under torture be
forgiven and rejoin the Church? What was to be
done with adulterers? Was property to be held in
common? Could Christians marry non-Christians?
Could they divorce? Remarry? How many times?
What about women? St Paul had written that
before God there was neither rich nor poor, nor
male nor female: how was this teaching to be put
into practice? Baptism washed away all past sins,
regardless: with baptism life started afresh. But
what if the baptised sinned again, after baptism?

Christians in the first century lived in the
conviction that the world as they knew it was soon
to end. Jesus had said, 'Behold I come soon'.
Marriage was therefore frowned upon and only to
be entered into – as St Paul preached – if sexual
temptation proved irresistible. Professional
ambition and political engagement were pointless.
Fasting and prayer, repentance for sins, good

deeds, renunciation of wealth: these defined the life of the serious Christian and the road to salvation. As the second century began, however, and then the third, and the world did not end after all, most Christians began to live by less stringent principles, buying and selling, embarking upon careers, pursing ambition for worldly office, marrying and raising children.

At this point, purists, dissatisfied with compromise or departure from the first Christian principles, as well as sensitive, spiritual persons disturbed by life in the grasping, noisy, often riotous cities, sought to remove themselves from the temptations of this world. In the third century both men and women started leaving civilisation's centres, particularly Alexandria in Egypt, to seek God in the wilderness of Judea, the Sinai and other desolate areas. There – alone as hermits or with a few like-minded souls – they lived lives of simplicity, self-denial, hardship and asceticism, fasting and praying for the sake of the riches of the spirit and the life to come. Thus monasticism began. The prototype of the monk was St Anthony (251–356 [!]), whose biography was written by his contemporary, St Athanasios, and whose temptations and torments by demons and monsters are a particularly popular subject for Western religious art.

As the fourth century began, Christians had good reason to be discouraged. Under the Emperor

⊙ *St Anthony the Great: a nineteenth-century household icon by an itinerant icon painter*

Diocletian, the full power of the state was focused on rooting them out. They were not permitted to hold public office or to serve in the army. If seeking public office and suspected of being Christian, they could be forced to prove they were not by performing pagan rites, such as sacrificing to

the emperor, one of the gods, or the Roman state.
If they refused, they could be tortured or killed.
If they went along with it and cooperated with the
authorities, they might well be permanently
excommunicated from their Church. The state
might also dispossess them, or banish them. They
were mocked as fools and fanatics, despised by the
cultured and elegant, ostracised from polite society.
Christians in the first, second and third centuries
took enormous risks and suffered terrible privations
and gruesome deaths for the sake of their faith.

Crisis: The Turning Point

At the same time, the direst prophesies seemed to
be coming true. At the close of the third century,
the barbarians began to press in on all sides of the
empire. As the invasions continued and intensified,
people came to believe that the world was coming
to an end, as indeed in a sense it was. (Eventually,
in 410, ancient Rome, the queen of cities and said
to be 1,162 years old, was to fall to the uncouth,
unknown and barbarian Goths, to struggle on its
knees for decades, and then to fall for good in 476,
when the last Roman emperor was forced to
abdicate.) The general chaos on the Italian
peninsula had repercussions throughout the
empire. The unthinkable seemed to be happening.
God was displeased with humankind. The long-
prophesied End of Days seemed at hand and the

time ripe for people to turn from worldly pursuits and dedicate themselves to reconciliation with God and the salvation of their souls. Some Roman citizens, convinced that the barbarians were succeeding precisely because the old gods were neglected, blamed the Christians. From 303 to 311, they rounded them up, drove them from their homes, mocked them and sent them to the public arenas to be devoured by wild animals for the diversion of the mob. Who would have thought that in only a few years the tables would be utterly, sweepingly, and permanently turned?

Yet this is what happened. In AD 313, the Edict of Milan granted Christians throughout the Roman Empire freedom from persecution. Christians emerged almost overnight from being a suspect and unsavoury minority meeting in caves and catacombs into the light of state protection and social approval, with magnificent structures – aglitter with gold and silver – in which to worship. This epochal turn of events was the work of Christianity's great champion, the Roman Emperor Constantine the Great: Orthodoxy's particularly beloved St Constantine.

Chapter 3

Constantine the Great

It can well be claimed that no one person has had so great an effect on the course of Western history as the Emperor Constantine (*c.* 272–337). It was he who put an end to the persecutions of the Christians by first declaring toleration of the new religion and then elevating it to be the imperially favoured religion of the Empire. His support for Christianity launched a revolution in the ancient world that set the direction of Western thought and belief for all of the centuries to follow, right down to our own time. Our laws, philosophy, codes of ethics and values – our architecture, art, literature and music – would not be what they are today if Constantine had not decided and acted as he did. Christianity is so integral to Western thought and culture that today – when it has largely slipped from the daily lives of vast numbers of Europeans and North Americans – we are not even conscious of its continuing impact on our lives. Yet in fact we all bear Constantine's heritage within us.

What made Constantine decide in favour of Christianity? None of the dozens of emperors between Augustus and himself had shown any

Christian inclinations. The new religion seemed to offer no political, social or economic advantages: it was a lesser faith, its predominantly poor and uneducated adherents making up an unknown number – but certainly only a small minority – of the empire's population in 313. Insisting as it did on its one God and its exclusive handle on truth, Christianity was an affront to the various religions to which most of the empire's people subscribed, including particularly

⊙ Constantine. Bronze head in the Capitoline Museum, Rome

the rich and powerful. Its focus on faith rather than reason offended thinking people and intellectual leaders in Constantinople (now Istanbul), Athens, Rome and Alexandria. It preached and practised equality of class and even gender: it was by nature socially revolutionary and potentially politically subversive. And it rejected almost everything that was fun – drunkenness, orgies, fighting, extra-marital sex, circuses – in favour of fasting, prayer, gentleness and love. It named God Himself and the human conscience as the ultimate authorities instead of the state and its leader, the emperor. So that in embracing Christianity, Constantine was effectively undermining his own position and power base.

There seem to be only two realistic explanations for his doing what he did, however implausible they may appear to us today. One was the influence of his mother, Helen; the other was his own character and personal experience. It is hard to imagine a brilliantly successful and overwhelmingly powerful head of state allowing either his mother or religious beliefs and superstitions to sway his policies. In Mediterranean cultures in particular, however, the mother–son relationship is arguably the most intimate, profound and enduring of all human relationships, and there is no reason to think that this was not true of Helen and Constantine – emperor or no. And in the fourth century, leaders often based their decisions on the prophesies of soothsayers and augurs: everyone at that time believed in the real and immediate presence and influence of the supernatural – in its various manifestations – at every turn. If we are to understand Constantine's motives, we must divest ourselves of the convictions and prejudices of our own time and not project them on to persons and events in the fourth century.

St Helen

Constantine's mother, Helen, was born in about AD 250, during the dark years of the mid-third-century Christian persecutions. The daughter of a provincial innkeeper, she came from Bithynia on the southern coast of the Black Sea. She was raised in the most humble and humbling circumstances, serving guests at her father's inn. At some point and for reasons we do not know, she became a devotee of the new religion, which she practised with ardour throughout her long life. Despite her initial position at the very bottom of the social ladder, she nevertheless – as was not entirely unusual in the socially fluid Byzantine Empire – became the wife of Constantius Chlorus, one of the greatest Roman generals of the day, who eventually became Emperor of the West. She bore Constantine to him in what is now Niš in Serbia on 27 February 272, historians more or less agree.

Once Constantine had grown up, served in the army all over Europe and been acclaimed emperor, he became justifiably suspicious of his near relatives, who in fact often plotted to overthrow him. Constantine was firm in cementing his position and had recourse to the methods of the day. He forced his father-in-law Maximian to commit suicide after uncovering his plot to seize power; he had his rebellious brother-in-law Licinius, his first wife Fausta and his illegitimate eldest son Crispus killed, apparently for conspiracy, and also his nephew Licianus. In his defence, it must be said that *Realpolitik* in Constantine's day was nothing for the delicate, and only a fool would free a conspirator. Amidst this intra-familial carnage, however, his mother remains without stain and accompanies him throughout his long career. Helen was the only indisputably and unquestioningly loyal intimate Constantine had throughout his life – and the only passionately devoted Christian believer in the family.

It has been argued that the relationship between Constantine and Helen could not have been close for the simple lack of a common language. Constantine made his career as a soldier: he spent his youth on campaign with his father in Western Europe. He therefore spoke Latin, the language of the government and army, while his mother spoke only Greek. This argument breaks down upon closer examination, however. He began life, after all, with his Greek-speaking mother. He certainly spoke at least some Greek and understood more – enough very probably to suffice for a warm bond with his mother. When he came to power, he was surrounded by Greek speakers and attended conferences at which the operating language was Greek. The fact that he made use of an interpreter does not mean he did not understand a good deal of Greek: an interpreter is a surety, and besides can be handily used to play for time during negotiations. It was at

Constantine's initiative that the Latin-speaking capital, Rome, was abandoned and Constantinople founded in the Greek-speaking eastern half of the empire. Constantine could not have instigated this daring shift unless he felt at ease in and sympathetic with his mother's Greek-speaking world and culture.

Helen was obviously a person of some character. Not only did she rise from the humble position of her birth to become the wife of a great general, she had the courage to embrace the new faith when it was still very dangerous to do so. Later, backed by her son's power, she practised her belief actively, founding orphanages, hospices and monasteries, and in the process winning the hearts of the empire's notably fickle population. Constantine opened the treasury to his mother's projects, and she backed the construction of innumerable churches, some of which are still standing, in whole or in part, today: the Church of the Nativity in Bethlehem, for example, the Church of the Burning Bush on Mount Sinai and the Ekatontapyliani on the island of Paros in Greece. Despite her advancing age and the perils and discomforts of the time, she undertook lengthy pilgrimages in search of holy relics: her efforts were crowned with the finding in Jerusalem of the cross upon which Jesus had been crucified. (According to legend, the fragrant basil plant was instrumental in revealing the site of the buried cross, growing persistently above it despite every effort by the pagans to uproot it. One often sees basil adorning icons in churches today.) Helen is reported to

⊙ *Icon of Saint Constantine and Saint Helen.*
Monastery at Shepherds' Field near Bethlehem

have died while on pilgrimage in Jerusalem and been
buried there.

Surely it is reasonable to assume that this devout,
resolute, unconventional, energetic, clever and long-
lived woman, over the years of close contact with her
son, exercised no mean influence on him, opening his
eyes and heart to Christianity. The Orthodox Church
links Saints Constantine and Helen closely: they are
celebrated together on 21 May.

'In This Sign Conquer'

In AD 312, Constantine had a powerful mystical
experience that seems to have swept him overnight
to the object of his inclinations. In 306, upon his
father's death in York, England, he had been
acclaimed Augustus by the army, cementing the
legitimacy of his claim to be emperor. Yet he was by
no means the only one. In 310, there were six other
claimants as well: Maximinus Daia in Syria; Galerius
in Thrace; Licinius in Pannonia and Rhaetia;
Maximianus in Gaul; Maxentius in Italy; and
Alexander in Africa. One by one they fell – or were
pushed – by the wayside, until Maxentius alone
remained to confront Constantine with an army in
the heart of the empire on the Italian peninsula.
The rival armies drew up opposite one another
at the Milvian Bridge near Rome. Maxentius and
his army were very powerful, the outcome was
uncertain, and everything hung in the balance. Just
before the decisive battle, as Constantine prayed for
divine guidance and support, the cross appeared to
him in the midday sky together with the message *In
hoc signo vince* – 'In this sign conquer'. Constantine
heeded the message. He bade his soldiers display the
cross on their arms, and went forth to victory. ICXC
NIKA – Greek for "Jesus [IC] Christ [XC] Conquers
[NIKA]" – appears everywhere in Orthodox churches
and iconography today, a constant reminder of
Emperor Constantine, the Church's great champion.

The Milvian Bridge experience was not Constantine's first vision. In 310, he had had a vision of Apollo, the Greek sun god, together with Victoria, the Roman goddess of victory. And Constantine – like many of the soldiers of his time – had also worshipped Sol Invictus, the unconquerable sun and source of light. The Christ of the Christians is called the Lord of Light and Light of Light. As an intelligent and civilised man of his era, Constantine believed in any case that all gods were manifestations of a single divine power. Before the great battle, he was no doubt highly sensitive and open to signs and wonders. And what could be a more convincing argument in favour of the new religion than victory?

Constantine was a politician and too canny to convert at once: if he had, he would surely have alienated his pagan subjects. Still, in gratitude for his triumph, he built the Lateran Basilica in Rome. For its part, the Roman Senate built him a triumphal arch with pagan elements, the sun god predominating as the supreme divinity in the text. Nevertheless, Constantine initiated a steady shift toward Christianity. In 313 he and his co-emperor Licinius promulgated the Edict of Milan, sealing the toleration of Christians and Christianity throughout the Roman Empire. From then on Christianity was secured: free to emerge from its caves and catacombs, to organise administratively, to build great structures, and to be practised in public. The

church of St. Peter in Rome was built in 324.
Between 331 and 334, Constantine closed down
many of the empire's pagan temples and shrines,
cults and oracles. By the end of the fourth century,
Christianity had become the state religion, with all
other religions outlawed.

Since at baptism new Christians are forgiven all
their sins, in the early days of Christianity converts
often put off this sacrament as long as possible,
prudently waiting until the last moment so as to
cover every eventuality and be forgiven every sin.
There was always the risk that sudden death might
catch them unawares, with all of their sins on their
heads, but they accepted the risk for the sake of the
blanket forgiveness that baptism ensured.
Constantine was one of these. For whatever reason
– personal or political – he put off baptism until he
lay on his deathbed in 337, when he was received
into the Church and absolved of a lifetime of sins.
And thus, duly penitent and graced with the
sacrament, Constantine entered God's kingdom and
eventually the ranks of the saints.

Constantine's decidedly bloody political
manoeuvring was common enough in his time and
indeed throughout history. Still, to our eyes political
assassination is difficult to reconcile with the
Christian spirit. Why was he made a saint? Persons
recognised by the Church as great Christians are
by no means free from flaw. Even St Peter thrice
denied Christ Himself, and St Paul vigorously

persecuted Christians before his conversion. The ranks of the saints include liars, cheats, drunkards, prostitutes, adulterers, etc. The Church seems to feel that it is the good that people do that counts most. Constantine's bold and firm support for Christianity – this daring and resolute shift of the foundations of the thousand-year-old Roman Empire, with its immense diversity of peoples and cultures – was the making of Christianity. From the Orthodox point of view, this was what counted in the end. Almost overnight Constantine provided Christianity with legitimacy and a world stage. To the Orthodox Church, the good he did was simply more important than his sins, however great. Because of Constantine, the Church was set on its way. Because of Constantine, the foundations and values of the Western world are Christian today.

Constantinople: The Christian Capital

We in the West are accustomed to viewing Rome as the Christian capital *par excellence*, but in this we err. For over a thousand years, it was unquestionably Constantinople that was the queen of cities, unsurpassed in beauty, magnificence, wealth, culture and religious grandeur. Despite Rome's thousand-year tradition, by the early fourth century, its days were numbered. Over the next few centuries, Goths, Visigoths, Vandals, Lombards and Slavs were to press in upon the empire from all

sides. Many of these 'barbarians' ultimately settled
within the empire and willingly adopted its
obviously superior ways, its 'civilisation', but before
they got that far, they posed a threat to the Roman
Empire generally and to the Italian peninsula in
particular. In retrospect, it is easy enough to see
what was happening. But considering Rome's claim
to be the 'eternal city', its venerable history and
seeming indestructibility under the protection of
the gods, one must credit Constantine with
amazing foresight in shifting the capital away to
the more defensible East.

In 330, he took the bold measure of setting up a
'New Rome' on the magnificent and impregnable
site of the little town of Byzantium on the Bosporus
between the Black Sea and the Sea of Marmara. He
measured out the city's dimensions in person, led,
he reported, by a guide visible only to himself. With
the unabashed self-assurance of the worldly great,
he named the city after himself: Constantinople,
that is, 'Constantine's city' or simply, as it was
known to the Greeks, *i polis* – The City. And so it
continues to be called even in our day, 'Istanbul'
being none other than the Turkish pronunciation of
the Greek *ees-teen-pol*, 'to The City'. The founding
of this city marked the beginning of what we now
know as the Byzantine Empire, and Constantinople
soon surpassed Rome in splendour.

Free of Rome's rooted pagan traditions – indeed
of any traditions whatever – Constantinople could

⊙ *Constantine presenting the city of Constantinople to the Mother of God and the Christ Child. Mosaic in Hagia Sophia, c.1000*

begin with a clean slate. It was from the start a Christian city and capital of the now Christian Roman Empire, the Byzantine Empire. At the same time it was Greek, and its rulers and population viewed it as the custodian of ancient Greek traditions in art, architecture and philosophy. The city was adorned with treasures from the ancient world garnered from all over the empire.

Over the centuries, Christian relics were also collected there. The most important was the True Cross upon which Jesus was crucified, which had been discovered by St Helen in Jerusalem. It was ultimately set up in Constantinople as the centre of the world, all distances throughout the empire being measured from it. Constantinople is to Eastern Orthodoxy what Rome is to Western Christianity. Many of the great monuments and churches built in the early years of Constantinople stand in Istanbul to this day: St Irene, SS Sergios and Bacchos, the great cisterns that provided the city with water, the giant walls surrounding the city, and above all the great church of St Sophia, completed in the sixth century, architecturally revolutionary with its wide-spanned, floating dome and still unsurpassed in many respects. St Sophia has – fortunately for its preservation – been declared a World Heritage Site, though in Muslim Turkey it no longer functions as a church.

Constantinople and the Byzantine Empire existed longer than any other empire in Western history: 1,123 years, from its founding in 330 to its fall to the Turks in 1453. Rome the ancient, the mother of cities, venerable Rome, always enjoyed the respect of the Byzantines, who indeed considered themselves to be 'Romans' and called themselves *Romaioi*. But as the fourth century became the fifth, and the fifth the sixth, Constantinople emerged as a glittering capital with a million inhabitants, while

Rome was overrun by barbarians, depopulated and left to go to ruin. And in Constantinople, the driving force for art and architecture, the guarantor of the city's safety in its most perilous hours, the arbiter of all issues – public and personal – was the new faith, championed by the Church.

In our democratic times, a clear division between Church and state is accepted as fundamental to guaranteeing freedom of conscience and tolerance. But people in the fourth century would not in the least have comprehended the logic of this division. If the truths of the Church were taken seriously – that there really is a God in heaven who loves humankind and sent His Son to save us and give us a code to live by and the prospect of eternal life – then the state must not only be in harmony with God and His Church but must ultimately exist only to serve them. The state and the Church were thus mutually dependent and indivisible in the minds of all people of that time. The state, people believed, could not even survive let alone flourish without the support and backing of God and His Church; and the Church depended upon the armies of the state to protect it from the invasions of barbarians and infidels. It also needed state support and funding for the rich surroundings appropriate to its dignity and to the creation of an inspiring setting for divine worship.

People at that time viewed the Roman/Byzantine Empire as the World, a complete entity, the cosmos.

(They knew, of course, of Africa and the East, but the world, to them, was their world, the civilised world, that is, the empire surrounding the Mediterranean Sea.) This world of theirs was logically to be modelled on the world above: Heaven. Like Heaven, it was to be governed by one great ruler, a king or queen who, if not a god, as in the past, was God's representative and could rule only by His grace. The Byzantines were by no means shocked to see their secular leader preside at Church councils, for example: on the contrary, they considered that consistent and God-fearing behaviour for a head of state. Truth, right and justice lay with God and the church that served him through *ortho doxy* – literally 'right belief/worship'. The state could only perform properly and successfully when in full harmony and close cooperation with the Church. Thus during periods of crisis the secular leadership ordered special worship and services to be held, and cities were renamed with Christian names. In processions, members of the military bore – as they still do today in Orthodox countries – icons through the streets of the capital. The relations between Church and state in many Orthodox countries today can only be grasped if the pervasiveness of this historical symbiosis of Church and state is understood.

Despite this holistic world view, however, the non-Christian barbarians continued to hammer at the gates, and their hammering became louder and

more persistent with the passage of time. After
Constantine, communications between Rome and
the rest of the empire began to break down and
came close to collapse with the rise of Islam. The
One World of the Roman Empire broke into two:
the Empire of the East, with Constantinople as its
capital, and the Empire of the West, with Rome.
The two-headed eagle that served as the emblem
of the new Roman Empire, the Byzantine Empire,
was thus both appropriate and prophetic. In the
end, East and West would have to go their separate
ways. Given the distances involved, the growing
difficulties and perils of travel and communication
from the fourth century on, and not least the
linguistic and intellectual division between the
Greek-speaking East and the Latin-speaking West,
the divide between East and West was inevitable.

Constantine was perhaps the last truly
cosmopolitan Roman emperor. He was born on the
cusp between East and West, in Niš in Serbia, on
the cultural divide that has remained so fatally prone
to political tremors right down to our own time.
Since his father was a general, Constantine spent his
young manhood with the army on the move in the
Western Roman provinces in Germany and Britain.
Throughout his life, there was quite clearly one
empire, one civilisation, one world. With its excellent
(for that time) communications and network of roads,
a cosmopolitanism that tolerated every sort of
person, race and culture, its unified administrative

and legal system, its two international languages, and, through Constantine, its single faith, the Byzantine Empire united and preserved the 'glory that was Greece and the grandeur that was Rome'. Constantine saw his empire as heir to both ancient Greece and ancient Rome, and himself as the steward and embodiment of both.

Thus at Constantine's death in 337, our shaky, squabbly, dogmatic, intolerant, visionary and revolutionary little Christian community had become an established, richly endowed, more-or-less consistent, state-supported and state-supporting institution. Towards the end of the fourth century the Emperor Theodosius the Great, who built the massive walls around Constantinople that stand in Istanbul to this day, granted Christianity a religious monopoly throughout the empire and banned all other religions. Orthodox Christianity was thus solidly established. And although during the next thousand years it to some extent shared the fortunes of its mother state, the Byzantine Empire, when Constantinople fell to the Muslim Turks in 1453, Orthodoxy lived on in the unconquerable hearts of the Orthodox faithful throughout Eastern and Balkan Europe and the vastnesses of Russia and eventually wherever they made their homes thereafter: in America, Canada, Western Europe, Australia, South Africa, Japan – everywhere in the world.

Chapter 4

Dogma and Belief

The Orthodox Church has come down to us fundamentally unchanged from Constantine's day. The doctrinal disputes that arose within it were resolved at Ecumenical Councils by bishops from all over the world, assembled in the presence of the Holy Spirit. The Nicene Creed, the resolutions of the seven great Councils held from the fourth to the eighth centuries, and the seven sacraments that eventually emerged in Church practice combine with Church tradition to form Orthodox dogma and reflect Orthodox belief.

The Seven Councils

From the start there was disagreement among Christians about basic issues. Jesus Christ: was he formed of a substance essentially divine, as the Monophysites claimed, or distinctly non-divine, as the Arians said? Was he a mixture of the two, or did he have two distinct natures? The Trinity: what was the constellation of relations between the Father, the Son and the Holy Ghost/Spirit? Did the Holy Spirit proceed from just the Father, as stated in the New Testament (John 15: 26), or did He proceed from the Father and the Son, as the *'filioque'* added to the Creed proclaimed? Priests: did sacraments performed by a sinful priest still count or were  they void, as the Donatists preached? Mary, Jesus' mother: was she a superior form of being, free of all blemish, singled out by God to bear his son, or was she a very pure and good but otherwise normal woman? Were two separate natures coexistent within the Son, so that Mary, as the Nestorians claimed, was the 'mother of Christ' only, and not the 'mother of God'? The ultimate power in the universe: was it all in God's hands or was it the object of continual struggle between the equally powerful forces of good and evil, as the Manicheans taught? Were people born good, as the Pelagians insisted, or were they tainted even at birth with original sin through the sexual act that had engendered them, as Augustine believed? And icons, that particularly incendiary issue: was it idolatrous to use them in worship, as the iconoclasts said, or correct, as the iconodules insisted?

In the third century – as Christians increased in number and their beliefs came to be more closely examined among both believers and non-believers – Christianity struggled to make itself clear and to determine what constituted orthodox (true) Christian belief and what did not, that is, what was heretical. To decide these issues, councils were held, attended by bishops from all over the empire, but primarily from the Eastern Empire, where the proceedings took place, in what is now Turkey. Representation from the West decreased as the Empire of the West gradually fell into the hands of the barbarians and disintegrated into chaos, and travel became ever more difficult and dangerous.

We need not attempt to explore here the rights and wrongs of the heresies, but if we are to understand the Orthodox Church, we must at least be aware of them. The Church's reaction to them determined the course of its history, and they explain the distinct existences of the Orthodox, Catholic, Coptic, Syrian Orthodox and other Churches today. The Seven Ecumenical Councils that dealt with the heresies form the bedrock of Orthodox belief. At that time, the word 'Ecumenical' did not have its present meaning of a conjunction of the various branches of Christianity: there were no such branches but only the One Church. Rather the word implied the inhabited earth – the whole civilised world: that is, the Roman/Byzantine Empire.

Each Council was called to deal with at least one heresy. Abstruse as these issues may appear even to many believing Christians today, they were of absolutely central significance to people at that time, who never doubted that their country's stability, their and their families' lives, happiness and even survival, their souls and their lives for all eternity hung in the balance. There was simply nothing more important to them, and they insisted that their Church and government, both, resolve such issues and behave consistently in ways pleasing to God, so that peace and prosperity would be assured in this world and salvation in the next.

Every issue was hotly debated not only by the finest minds of the day but in fact by virtually everyone. In the fourth century, Gregory of Nyssa, one of the great Church Fathers, complained, 'If you ask for some change, you get a philosophy concerning the begotten and unbegotten. If you ask the price of a loaf of bread, the baker declares that the Father is greater and the Son less. If you want to know if your bath is ready, you are answered that the Son was created from nothing.'

Scores of Councils met to decide such questions. The great Councils were presided over by the Roman – that is, the Byzantine – emperor, who after 324 resided in Constantinople. Not being a member of the clergy, the emperor did not generally participate in the debate and treated the participants with deference, but – motivated by a desire for peace and harmony within the empire – he did not hesitate to remove and banish any particularly recalcitrant bishops who threatened to obstruct consensus. Those who refused to fall in line were declared heretics and excommunicated from the Church. Seven Councils – all held at sites in what is today Turkey – are recognised by the Orthodox Church as authoritative for Orthodox belief. Although the issues raised at the Councils are far too complex to be explored in any depth here, at least a brief summary is indispensable to an understanding of the Eastern Church, even at the risk of some omission or oversimplification.

At the First Council in Nicaea, in 325, three hundred and eighteen bishops assembled from all over the empire. With Constantine himself presiding, they composed and decided the bulk of what is now known as the Nicene Creed. Debate hinged particularly on the Greek word describing the Father and Son: were these two persons in the Trinity *homoousios* (of the *same* substance) or *homoiousios* (of *like* substance)? The Council ultimately resolved that the Son was of the *same* substance as the Father, rejecting as heresy the position of Arius that their substances were merely *like* to one another. It was assisted in reaching this conclusion by Constantine himself, whose patience was tried by what he saw as hair-splitting. As we

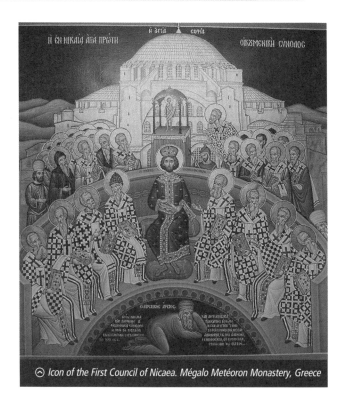

⊙ *Icon of the First Council of Nicaea. Mégalo Metéoron Monastery, Greece*

know, Constantine was a soldier and man of action; his native language was not Greek but Latin. At a certain point, he refused to listen to further debate about the pesky and in his view insignificant Greek *iota*. And so it was eliminated and the Father and Son declared to be *homoousios* – and that was that.

Considering the complexity of the theological issues involved and the philosophical and linguistic

diversity of the assembled bishops, the fact that
communication was possible and agreement
eventually reached is something of a miracle in
itself. That the three hundred and eighteen learned,
opinionated, passionate, strong-willed and wily
members of this Council managed to agree on a
creed attests as nothing else could to the great
power of the Holy Spirit among them. As later
finalised, the Nicene Creed is a plain, brief and
forthright statement of what all Orthodox believe.

The Second Council was held in Constantinople
in 381. This Council completed the Creed in the
final form printed opposite, excluded from the
Church anyone who would not subscribe to it and
declared Constantinople the leading site in the
Eastern Church, second in honour only to Rome. As
did the Council of Nicaea, it definitively condemned
Arianism, which taught that Jesus was not fully
divine in nature, though this resilient heresy
continued to be popular and sprang up again
among the Goths in the West.

The Third Ecumenical Council in 431 was held
in Ephesus, on the western coast of Turkey, in the
great church dedicated to the Virgin Mary whose
foundations may still be seen there today. It
declared against Nestorianism, confirming Christ to
be a single being, both divine and human, and his
mother, Mary, thus to warrant the title 'mother of
God' and not merely 'mother of Christ', because she
bore God as a man. The Nestorians ultimately

» The Nicene Creed

I believe in one God, Father, Almighty, Maker of Heaven and Earth and of all things visible and invisible.

And in One Lord Jesus Christ, the Only-Begotten Son of God, begotten of the Father before all Ages. Light of Light, True God of True God, begotten not made, One in essence with the Father, through Whom all things were made.

Who for us human beings* and for our salvation came down from Heaven, and was incarnated by the Holy Spirit and of the Virgin Mary, and became Man.

And was crucified for us under Pontius Pilate, suffered and was buried.

And rose on the third day according to the Scriptures.

And ascended into Heaven, and sitteth at the right hand of the Father.

And He shall come again with glory to judge the living and the dead; Whose Kingdom shall have no end.

And in the Holy Spirit, the Lord, the Giver of Life, Who proceedeth from the Father, Who with the Father and the Son together is worshipped and glorified; Who spoke by the Prophets.

In One Holy, Catholic and Apostolic Church.

I acknowledge One Baptism for the remission of sins.

I look for the resurrection of the dead.

And the life of the age to come. Amen.†

*The Greek word '*anthropous*' is best translated by 'human beings', rather than 'men'.
† *The Divine Liturgy Explained*, by Revd Nicholas M. Elias, Astir Publishers, Athens, 1984, 4th ed.

withdrew altogether from the Church and moved out of the empire to Persia – to parts of modern Iran and Iraq – where their descendants live to this day.

The Fourth Council, held in Chalcedon in 451, declared that Christ was one person with two natures, both human and divine, united 'without confusion, separation, division or change' – a rejection of the popular Eastern heresy of Monophysitism, which claimed Christ's nature to be one, solely divine. It also declared the Bishop of Constantinople to be second in honour only to the Bishop of Rome, the Pope.

The Fifth Council in 553 – the second to be held in Constantinople – condemned Nestorian tendencies within the Church once more, attempting but failing to mollify the Monophysites, who ultimately broke away from the Orthodox Church to found the Jacobite Church in Syria and the Coptic Church in Egypt. This was a great loss to Orthodoxy, since when the Arabs invaded nearly a century later, many of the kindred Egyptians found the simplicity of the concept of God in Islam more attractive than the Christian complexities of the Trinity. Over the course of the centuries, as many Muslims settled in Egypt, Egyptian Christians also converted, so that only a small Christian minority lives within the Muslim state of Egypt today.

The Sixth Council was held in 680–1 in Constantinople to reinstate the doctrines of the two energies and two wills of Father and Son and condemn Monothelitism, a compromise doctrine which had been suggested in hopes of unifying the discordant Christians but had instead only fired further debate. Monothelitism suggested that Christ had but one divine will, although he had a human and divine nature. It was never a particularly popular concept.

The final Council, the seventh, held in 787 in Nicaea like the first, was called to deal with the emotionally highly charged issue of holy images, over which Eastern Christians were deeply divided (unlike their Western brethren, who with few exceptions were little troubled by the issue and favoured images). Particularly those parts of the empire farthest to the East and bordering on the Islamic and Monophysite regions tended to oppose as idolatry the use of images in Orthodox worship. Those against the use of icons in worship were called *iconoclasts,* or 'icon-breakers'; those in favour were called *iconodules,* or 'icon-reverers'. Emotions ran very high between the two. When the eighth-century iconoclast Emperor Leo III commanded that the icon of Christ over the gates of his palace in Constantinople be destroyed, the unfortunate officer commissioned with the task was killed by a mob of furious women.

For the better part of a hundred years the issue of iconoclasm was hotly argued, with first one side, then the other, gaining the ascendancy. Iconoclast

emperors alternated with iconodules, and their
bureaucracies – and thus the entire machinery of
the state – more or less followed their lead.
Everyone was directly affected by the issue, which
determined everyday prayer and religious practice.
The iconoclasts argued that to pray before icons
amounted to idolatry. The iconodules countered
that *adoration* was for God alone, but that images
of holy personages could and should be *revered*:
that they were an aid to worship for the faithful.
They maintained, besides, that since all of the
saints, the Virgin Mary and Christ himself had had
human form, to represent them assisted the faithful
and directed their prayers to the icon's prototype.
Even angels, they pointed out, had been seen by
human beings. They went on to argue that it was
not after all the physical object itself – the painted
wood – that was reverenced, but the personage
and holiness represented. For ordinary people, the
shift from pagan worship of various idols and
objects to holy images was free of these
compunctions and complications and was thus
particularly facilitated. Holy images were credited
with countless miracles, including saving
Constantinople from invasion on more than one
occasion. As we see in Orthodox churches
throughout the world, the iconodules won the day –
to the joy of the Orthodox and art-lovers
everywhere. The Council of Nicaea of 787, which
decided in favour of icons, was the last great

Council to be recognised by the Eastern Orthodox Church, and dogma has not changed since.

The long-running controversy about icons had profound geopolitical consequences. The Byzantines were so passionately embroiled in the icon debate that they failed to respond to the desperate appeals of Pope Stephen II (752–7) to send armies to drive the barbarian Lombards, who were threatening Rome itself, out of the Italian peninsula. In a bold move that altered forever the balance of power within the empire and the course of European history as well, Pope Stephen crossed the Alps in the dead of winter in 753–4 to appeal instead to the king of the Franks, Pippin. Pippin responded where the Byzantines had not, and in return for the significant act of papal anointment as King, came to the Pope's defence. Thus the Bishop of Rome, the Pope, came to assume a major role in Western politics, and the wedge of language, geography, religion and culture was driven deeper than ever between East and West – as it turned out, irreversibly. Virtually unnoticed, East and West split at this point for good.

The Seven Sacraments

Orthodox worship involves seven sacraments: baptism, chrismation, confession, communion, matrimony, ordination, and unction. These sacraments define the individual's life within the

Church and mark important stages in the personal lives of every Orthodox Christian. They are joyful but very serious events, conducted by ordained members of the clergy in the presence of the community of the faithful and the Holy Spirit. The sacraments are based on scripture, the writings of the Church Fathers, and Church tradition.

A sacrament might be called 'a sacred act that confers grace', but further definition would be out of place in Orthodoxy. The word 'act' should be stressed, for the sacraments were intended to be used – to bestow grace – not to be defined or artificially constricted as dogma. Consequently no Orthodox Ecumenical Council has pronounced upon the nature of sacraments, or attempted to define their essentially indefinable nature: they have been left free to unfold their effects as the Spirit ordains.

The sacrament that initiates a person into the Christian Church is **Baptism**. During baptism the candidate – usually these days a baby – joins the community of Christians through immersion in water by a priest in the name of the Father, and the Son, and the Holy Ghost. This sacrament is, with communion, one of the two oldest, being described in the New Testament and in Christian writings as early as the first century. It is in imitation of Christ's own baptism in the Jordan river by St John, as related in the New Testament. With baptism, new Christians are forgiven all sins and make a fresh start in life. Their godfather or godmother is bound to them by a profound, life-long tie and is responsible for the godchild's spiritual development and general well-being. The godchild may always turn to them as to his or her own parents. In early Christianity, many people did not become Christians until they were adults, which is why baptismal fonts from those days are often quite commodious and set low or in the ground. Adults nowadays are sometimes baptised in the sea. As prescribed in the Creed, baptism may not be repeated.

In the Orthodox Church, the sacrament of **Chrismation** ('confirmation' in the West) immediately follows baptism, on the same occasion, whereas in the Western Churches it does not take place until the candidate 'attains the age of reason'. In Eastern Orthodoxy, it is not considered essential for a person to be able to reason to be accepted into full Church membership, since reason is not definitive in the soul's health and salvation, which are open to all, including people who are mentally undeveloped or incapacitated. During chrismation the candidate is anointed with oil, which is a substitute for the laying on of hands by the Apostles and their successors, the bishops. As such, this special oil must be blessed and prepared by either a patriarch or synod of bishops, whose authority is derived through an unbroken line of laying on of hands from the Apostles themselves and thus from Christ Himself. At the same time, a tuft of hair is cut in a symbolic tonsure, an act of self-consecration to God. Christian converts to Orthodoxy undergo chrismation.

At the close of the chrismation service, in some parishes, the new Orthodox Christian may be presented to the congregation: 'Is s/he worthy?' asks the priest. 'Worthy!' cry the assembled people. 'Is s/he worthy?' asks the priest again. 'Worthy!' they cry. 'Is s/he worthy?' asks the priest a third time for good measure. 'Worthy!' everyone shouts, accepting the person as a new member of the Christian community. As always, the community of Orthodox is called upon as a whole; and as always with important points, the question is asked three times.

Orthodox believers go to **Confession** whenever they have committed actions or had thoughts they feel to be wrong, so that their souls are oppressed. They usually confess one to four times a year. The Greek word for 'sin' is *amartia*, which has a somewhat different connotation from the English word 'sin'. It means literally *a missing of the mark*, as an archer might fail to hit the target. The sacrament clears penitents' way to hit the mark once more and proceed with their lives unburdened. It also prepares them to receive the Eucharist with a glad heart, as prescribed in I John 1: 'If we say that we have no sin, we deceive ourselves . . . If we confess our sins, he [Jesus Christ] is faithful and just to forgive us our sins and to cleanse us from all unrighteousness.'

The confession is made to an ordained priest or monk, often but not necessarily in a church. Priest and penitent confront one another face-to-face. In the nature of a serious talk between friends, the penitent tells the priest what they feel they have done wrong, which of their thoughts they consider unworthy, or what is troubling their soul. The priest may then ask them questions to elucidate their situation, and the two discuss the problem until it is clear. The priest then gives advice on how to get back on course, and may suggest actions the penitent must take. In Orthodoxy, such counsel tends to be pragmatic rather than dogmatic: it is a sincere attempt to help individual Christians come to terms with specific circumstances in the real world in ways consistent with Christian love. The penitent then kneels before the priest, who covers his or her head with his stole, the symbol of his priestly power, and prays that Christ may forgive the penitent and grant His blessing and aid.

The sacrament of **Communion** was inaugurated by Christ himself at his last supper with his disciples when he '. . . took bread, and blessed it, and brake it, and gave it to the disciples, and said, Take, eat; this is my body. And he took the cup, and gave thanks, and gave it to them, saying, Drink ye all of it; For this is my blood of the new testament, which is shed for many for the remission of sins.' (See Chapter 7: Visiting an Orthodox Church.) These actions are now repeated in remembrance of Him. Of the seven sacraments, baptism and communion are the oldest: Christ himself was

⊙ *Iconostasis in a Greek village church with a priest preparing the service*

baptised by St John, and he initiated communion at the Last Supper. Through the power of the Holy Spirit, invoked by the priest, Jesus is believed to be present in the bread that is his body and in the wine that is his blood, in a manner that the senses cannot detect or the mind understand. It is a profound mystery. When the communicants partake of the bread and wine, Jesus thus enters into their bodies, hearts and souls to pervade their entire beings. The Orthodox credit this sacrament with every kind of healing power and wish their friends who have just taken communion, 'May it help you!' It is considered especially important that children partake of communion to strengthen and protect

them against every ill. Adults prepare themselves
for communion with prayer and strict fasting.

A particularly joyous sacrament is **Matrimony**,
filled as it is with both human and divine love,
joining together of the man and woman to complete
one another, and auguring hope and happiness for
the future, the birth of children and the continuation
of the human race. The ceremony has two simple
components: the declaration of the bride and groom
that they are entering this union of their own free
will, without constraint; and the uniting of the two
by the priest with the words 'The servant of God
[groom] is espoused to the handmaiden of God
[bride] in the name of the Father and of the Son and
of the Holy Spirit. Amen.' In the Orthodox service,
they are crowned with marriage wreaths which are
tied together with a ribbon and switched back and
forth between their two heads. Another feature of
this service is a formal but joyful dance around the
table which has been placed before the holy gates
at the midpoint of the iconostasis, led by the priest
and followed by the bride and groom. At this point
the congregation throw rice for the couple's good
fortune and happiness. According to folk custom,
whichever partner steps on the other's foot at this
time will dominate in the marriage!

Marriage may take place between Orthodox and
non-Orthodox but is discouraged. Divorce is
possible in Orthodoxy but is viewed with sorrow
and regret by the Orthodox. In the Gospel

according to Matthew we read, 'What therefore God hath joined together let not man put asunder . . . Moses because of the hardness of your hearts suffered you to put away your wives: but from the beginning it was not so.' The Orthodox may marry three times – not more for any reason. Second or third marriages are conducted on a more sombre, less celebratory note. Priests may marry only once, before ordination.

Ordination is the sacrament that qualifies men – and only men – as bishops or priests, so that they may administer the sacraments to Orthodox believers, and either men or women as deacons. This sacrament may be performed only by a bishop, through the laying on of hands and prayers invoking the grace of the Holy Spirit. At this sacrament, the officiating bishop asks the assembled congregation, 'Is he worthy?' To which the people usually reply, 'He is worthy!' If a cry of 'not worthy' is heard, the proceedings are interrupted, and the objection is carefully investigated. A bishop or priest is not forced upon a flock who do not want him.

Unction is the sacrament performed for the health of body and soul. It is drawn from the epistle of St James: 'Is someone sick among you? Let him bring in the priests of the church; and let them pray over him, anointing him with oil in the name of the Lord: And the prayer of faith shall save the sick person, and the Lord shall raise him up; and if he

has committed sins, they shall be forgiven him.'
Unction should be preceded by confession and
followed by communion. The essential parts of the
ceremony are the anointing of participants with
consecrated oil and the prayers for the restoration or
preservation of health of body and soul.

Belief in Everyday Terms

Eastern Orthodox belief is in the main the same
belief that all Christians share. Still, the emphasis
in the various Churches does differ significantly.
Orthodoxy stresses the resurrection rather than the
crucifixion: Christ resurrected rather than Christ
crucified. Certainly the cross is everywhere to be
seen in Orthodoxy – at the throat or breast of every
Orthodox believer, for instance, atop the centre of
the iconostasis, upon every church. Still, the
Orthodox do not so often wear crosses with the
body of Christ crucified. The pervasiveness and
importance of Christ's resurrection is especially
clear in a Greek Orthodox tradition during the forty
days between Easter and the Ascension. Instead of
greeting one another with 'hello' or 'good day',
good Orthodox say to one another in the street or at
the supermarket, 'Christ is risen!' to which the
reply comes, 'Indeed, he is risen!'

Orthodox do share the common Christian
conviction that as human beings they are imperfect,
but not the specifically Augustinian view that each

person is born in a sinful state traceable to Adam's fall or sexual congress. The concept of Original Sin would be understood by the Orthodox as simply the fallibility of human nature. Humans are not perfect: they are born with weaknesses and imperfections with which they must contend. The aim of the devout Orthodox life is not primarily the negative effort to rid ourselves from sin but the positive effort to attain *theosis* – to become deified ourselves by living out God within us.

Added to this is the encouraging and profound conviction that God really does love us all, that we are His creatures, despite our failings – that not one of us is not lovable. The Orthodox recognise their human imperfections, but they accept their inevitability. They feel that God loves us, warts and all. This conviction gives the Orthodox great inner confidence. They are not generally haunted by a struggle with guilt. One indication of this is confession, which in Orthodoxy is an attempt of the individual to free him or herself of a fault that is a burden and is keeping them from 'moving on'. The priest does not absolve the penitent of guilt: rather, he serves as the penitent's guide and counsellor and – as an expert in matters of human error and repentance – prays with and for him or her to find release.

Orthodoxy is permeated with associations from nature, in which believers everywhere see God's hand: the source of light, the sun, is praised with Christ every evening at vespers. Wheat, representing regeneration, is served at memorial services for the dead. Bread, wine and olive oil are blessed regularly as the fundamental nourishment that sustains us all. Vines, grapes and vine leaves, recalling Christ's words 'I am the true vine', twine about various items in any church. Church décor often displays natural elements, sometimes erroneously interpreted by art historians and critics as pagan. Psalm 103 (104 in Western numbering*), read every evening of the year except Great (Good) Friday and during the week after Easter, is nothing less than a long and detailed hymn of praise for the natural wonders God has created, in which human beings may and should delight. The translation below is from the Septuagint, the version of the Old Testament accepted by the Orthodox.

*The King James version of the Old Testament separates Psalm 9 of the Septuagint into Psalms 9 and 10 and combines Psalms 146 and 147 into Psalm 147. This means that Psalms 10 to 147 in the King James are one number higher than as numbered in the Septuagint used by the Orthodox.

» Psalm 103

Bless the Lord, O my soul. O Lord my God, thou art very great; thou hast clothed thyself with praise and honour:

Who dost robe thyself with light as with a garment; spreading out the heaven as a curtain.

Who covers his chambers with waters; who makes the clouds his chariot; who walks on the wings of the wind. Who makes his angels spirits, and his ministers a flaming fire.

Who establishes the earth on her sure foundation: it shall not be moved for ever.

The deep, as it were a garment, is his covering: the waters shall stand on the hills.

At thy rebuke they shall flee; at the voice of thy thunder they shall be alarmed.

They go up to the mountains, and down to the plains, to the place which thou hast founded for them.

Thou hast set a bound which they shall not pass, neither shall they turn again to cover the earth.

He sends forth his fountains among the valleys: the waters shall run between the mountains.

They shall give drink to all the wild beasts of the field: the wild asses shall take of them to quench their thirst.

By them shall the birds of the sky lodge: they shall utter a voice out of the midst of the rocks.

He waters the mountains from his chambers: the earth shall be satisfied with the fruit of thy works.

He makes grass to grow for the cattle, and green herb for the service of men, to bring bread out of the earth;

and wine makes glad the heart of man, to make his face cheerful with oil: and bread strengthens man's heart.

The trees of the plain shall be full of sap; even the cedars of Libanus which he has planted.

There the sparrows will build their nests; and the house of the heron takes the lead among them.

The high mountains are a refuge for the stags, and the rock for the rabbits.

He appointed the moon for seasons: the sun knows his going down.

Thou didst make darkness, and it was night; in it all the wild beasts of the forest will be abroad: even young lions roaring for prey, and to seek meat for themselves from God.

The sun arises, and they shall be gathered together, and shall lie down in their dens.

Man shall go forth to his work, and to his labour till evening.

How great are thy works, O Lord! in wisdom hast thou wrought them all: the earth is filled with thy creation.

So is this great and wide sea: there are things creeping innumerable, small animals and great.

There go the ships; and this dragon whom thou hast made to play in it.

All wait upon thee, to give them their food in due season.

When thou hast given it them, they will gather it; and when thou hast opened thine hand, they shall all be filled with good.

But when thou hast turned away thy face, they shall be troubled: thou wilt take away their breath, and they shall fail, and return to their dust.

Thou shalt send forth thy Spirit, and they shall be created; and thou shalt renew the face of the earth.

Let the glory of the Lord be for ever: the Lord shall rejoice in his works;

who looks upon the earth, and makes it tremble; who touches the mountains, and they smoke.

I will sing to the Lord while I live; I will sing praise to my God while I exist.

Let my meditation be sweet to him: and I will rejoice in the Lord.

Let the sinners fail from off the earth, and transgressors, so that they shall be no more. Bless the Lord, O my soul.

'O LORD, how manifold are thy works!' says the psalmist. 'In wisdom hast thou made them all: the earth is full of thy riches.' With this view of all nature as God's own work, it is small wonder that so many Orthodox bishops and monasteries were especially quick to embrace environmentally friendly practices when it became clear that people are destroying God's creation through carelessness and ignorance. The present Ecumenical Patriarch, His All Holiness Bartholomew, Archbishop of Constantinople and New Rome, has earned the title 'the Green Patriarch'.

⊙ *The Ecumenical Patriarch Bartholomew*

Orthodox belief tends to be intuitive rather than reasoned out, the result of synthesis rather than analysis. Although there have indeed been many and profound Orthodox thinkers and theologians, the Orthodox do not tend to debate the fine points of their religion, to analyse and break down. In fact, Orthodox theology and Orthodox religious practice are not considered separately from one another. Orthodox belief is accessible to anyone – little children and the mentally retarded, too – because it is conveyed not entirely by words and the intellect but also by symbols and ritual, which circumvent the mind, leave considerable latitude to each individual, and touch people in their hearts. The Orthodox often mention the heart specifically as the centre of prayer and the truest counsellor for good decisions.

Despite the controversies over heresy in the early centuries, Orthodoxy did not go through the intense intellectual theological analysis of the medieval scholastic period in the West. It is a religion more of the spirit than of the mind, of symbol and ritual more than exegesis, of tradition rather than of dogma or prescribed rules. Part of this distinction hinges on a very important word that does not exist in English and whose original meaning and connotations in Greek are not translatable: the *Logos*. The translation into English as 'Word' has created much confusion and misunderstanding. *Logos* means: 'meaning', 'message', 'reason', 'purpose', 'cause', 'significance' and much more all rolled up into one:

not just 'word'. Jesus is the *Logos*, the personification of *meaning*, God's very message. In English when we read in the Gospel of St John, 'In the beginning was the Word', we should be reading, 'In the beginning was the *Logos*' – a far broader, more complex and more profound concept than what 'Word' conveys in any but a very artificial and academic sense. The *Logos* cannot ultimately be approached through reason and words – the media of the mind – without the media of the spirit: symbol and ritual.

Likewise, Orthodox avoid speculation about God's nature, since any such speculation would inevitably be in human terms and therefore limited and hopelessly skewed. This is where what is called the *apophatic* form of theology comes into play: a human being may reasonably claim to know what God *is not*, but is far too limited to know what God is. The only positive statements regularly made about God are that he is holy, mighty, and immortal.

Orthodox Christians believe that God exists in three persons, bound together in love. These are the Father (the creator of all), the Son (Jesus Christ) and the Holy Spirit or Holy Ghost. No person has ever seen the Father, who is the author or source of the world around us, the universe, and the unseen world of spirits and thoughts. The Holy Spirit abides among us and is there when we call upon Him to be our comforter: He imbues all things everywhere and is ever-present. Jesus Christ is the

Son of God, God in human form. He came to live among us in Palestine two thousand years ago, and He lives on today among us, unseen, along with the Father and the Holy Spirit. God sent Him to us so that we might have before us a model of human perfection and redeem ourselves from ignorance and despair. He was miraculously born of a virgin but nonetheless human mother named Mary, whom God chose for her particular purity to give His son human form. The Orthodox especially honour Mary, the God-Bearer or Mother of God, as the vessel for the incarnation of God, the medium for God's humanity, and thus the means through which we can know God and save ourselves.

Prayers

Among the prayers central to Orthodox belief and practice, five might be cited in particular.

Kyrie eleison, the shortest, is the abbreviated Greek form of 'Lord Jesus Christ, son of God, have mercy on me, a sinner.' The *Kyrie eleison* is also used as an aid to enlightenment in Orthodox mystical practice, in which it is repeated inwardly to the rhythm of breathing. Thus the practitioner prays without ceasing, as St Paul bade us, while breathing in and out. The phrase is also common in Western religious services.

'Holy God, Holy Mighty, Holy Immortal: have mercy upon us!' is the thrice-holy hymn to God and

is as specific a statement as the Orthodox generally care to make about the nature of God. The prayer particularly establishes the relationship between God and the worshipper.

The Lord's Prayer (see Chapter 1: Jesus' Life), taught us by Christ Himself, is used throughout the Christian world. It is a fine summary of our most essential needs, those that we particularly ask God in his mercy to fulfil.

The prayer-hymn to the Holy Spirit is a plea that He may fill us with His good spirit and be with us always:

Heavenly King, Comforter, Spirit of Truth,
everywhere present and filling all things,
Treasury of the Good and Donor of Life: come,
dwell within us; and cleanse us of all stain;
and, O Kindly One, save our souls.

Psalm 50 (51 Western) is particularly important to Orthodox meditation. It is repeated in every liturgy.

These prayers have subtle differences in different languages, with significant implications for belief. As mentioned earlier in this chapter, 'sin' in Greek *amartia*, is not quite the same as 'sin' in the English sense but rather a missing of the mark, so that 'sinners' are people who have not succeeded in doing what they should rather than specifically doing what they should not. Likewise the word 'have mercy on' – *eleison* in Greek –

means 'to bestow bounty on' as well as 'to be merciful to'. So that the first prayer, the *Kyrie eleison*, has a slightly different cast in Greek from that of its usual English translation.

But perhaps the greatest, most perfect form of prayer of all is wordless. It is, as Metropolitan Kallistos Ware has written, the encounter between God and man in the kingdom of the heart. This is the most difficult kind of prayer to practise – to empty one's mind of the hodgepodge of thoughts and chatter that fill it and to attend upon God Himself: not always to pour out one's own thoughts incessantly into God's ear, as it were, but to open heart and mind and *listen* with one's soul. To pray in this manner requires determination, focus and practice, but it is the most rewarding prayer of all – the most comforting and satisfying – since to pray in this way is to communicate with God.

» Psalm 50

Have mercy upon me, O God, according to thy great mercy; and according to the multitude of thy compassions blot out my transgression.

Wash me thoroughly from mine iniquity, and cleanse me from my sin.

For I am conscious of mine iniquity; and my sin is continually before me.

Against thee only have I sinned, and done evil before thee: that thou mightest be justified in thy sayings, and mightest overcome when thou art judged.

For, behold, I was conceived in iniquities, and in sins did my mother conceive me.

For, behold, thou lovest truth: thou hast manifested to me the secret and hidden things of thy wisdom.

Thou shalt sprinkle me with hyssop, and I shall be purified: thou shalt wash me, and I shall be made whiter than snow.

Thou shalt cause me to hear gladness and joy: the afflicted bones shall rejoice.

Turn away thy face from my sins, and blot out all mine iniquities.

Create in me a clean heart, O God; and renew a right spirit in my inward parts.

Cast me not away from thy presence; and remove not thy holy Spirit from me.

Restore to me the joy of thy salvation: establish me with thy directing Spirit.

Then will I teach transgressors thy ways; and ungodly men shall turn to thee.

Deliver me from blood-guiltiness, O God, the God of my salvation: and my tongue shall joyfully declare thy righteousness.

O Lord, thou shalt open my lips; and my mouth shall declare thy praise.

For if thou desiredst sacrifice, I would have given it: thou wilt not take pleasure in whole-burnt-offerings.

Sacrifice to God is a broken spirit: a broken and humbled heart God will not despise.

Do good, O Lord, to Sion in thy good pleasure; and let the walls of Jerusalem be built.

Then shalt thou be pleased with a sacrifice of righteousness, offering, and whole-burnt-sacrifices: then shall they offer calves upon thine altar.

Chapter 5

The Christian Year

Easter and the Twelve Great Feasts

During the course of the year, Orthodox Christians celebrate twelve great holy days, some of which are holidays throughout the Western world, plus Easter, the 'feast of feasts'. Each marks a major event in the life of Jesus Christ or his holy mother, the Virgin Mary. These occasions are the subject of much of the great art in both East and West. Familiarity with them thus helps us to understand both Christian practice and centuries of religious painting, poetry, drama and music. They are important events in the life of Orthodox communities and are repeatedly recalled in iconography. The great feasts mark the passage of the year in the established rhythm of Christ's life, tying each Christian life to His own.

In Orthodoxy, Easter (celebrated in April or May), the 'feast of feasts', is the most important occasion in the Church year – too special to be numbered on a par with other feasts. Easter celebrates the great miracle of Christ's resurrection from the dead, the fulfilment of God's promise that if we believe in Him we will not die but will have eternal life. The date of **Easter** – *Pascha* or the **Anastasis** – in both the Eastern Orthodox Church and the Western Churches is the first Sunday after the first full moon after the vernal equinox. However, when it comes to Easter, the Orthodox Church uses the Julian calendar introduced by Julius Caesar in 46 BC. This calendar is now thirteen days behind the more solarly accurate Gregorian calendar introduced by Pope Gregory XII in 1582 and adopted piecemeal throughout the world from the sixteenth to the twentieth centuries. According to the Julian calendar, the vernal equinox is 3 April, so the date of Easter in the Orthodox Church is based on that. Thus, depending on the date of the full moon, Orthodox Easter sometimes coincides with Western Easter, sometimes not. (See page 164 for the dates of Easter in the Eastern and Western Churches in coming years.)

Because of the lunar factor, Easter is a 'moveable feast', celebrated at a different date each year. Since three of the twelve great feasts are tied to Easter, they, too, are moveable. The remaining nine feasts have set dates. Let us start with those. (Dates according to the Gregorian calendar in common use throughout the world today.)

Christ's life as a man began nine months in advance of Christmas, the date of His birth, when the angel Gabriel appeared to Mary and said to her, 'Behold, thou shalt conceive in thy womb, and bring forth a son, and shalt call his name Jesus. He shall be great, and shall be called the Son of the Highest.' Upon which Mary responded, 'How shall this be, seeing I know not a man?' And the angel said, 'The Holy Ghost shall come upon thee, and the power of the Highest shall overshadow thee: therefore also that holy thing which shall be born of thee shall be called the Son of God . . . For with God nothing shall be impossible.' And Mary freely acquiesced in what God proposed to her, saying 'Behold the handmaid of the Lord; be it unto me according to thy word.' This event is the **Annunciation**, celebrated on 25 March.

Christmas is the one feast surely everyone – Christian and non-Christian – knows and understands, even though its true meaning has been virtually quashed by the commercial behemoth of consumption and kitsch that accompanies it today. It is celebrated in the Greek, Romanian and Bulgarian Orthodox Churches, for instance, on 25 December, just as in the Western Churches. Other Orthodox Churches, however – for instance the Russian and Serbian Orthodox Churches – still use the Julian calendar, which would put Christmas on 7 January. Christmas celebrates the birth of Jesus in Bethlehem to Mary, the espoused wife of Joseph. On this occasion, the light of love and divine understanding entered the world, as God Himself took human form as Jesus Christ, to live among us, guide us and give us hope.

On 2 February, the 'churching' of the baby Jesus and his mother is celebrated as the **Presentation of Christ** – forty days following his birth, as is the custom to this day in Orthodoxy. By that time, the baby and mother are considered strong enough to come to the church and be (re)introduced to it by the priest (see Chapter 1: Jesus' Life).

On 6 January, **Theophany** (the manifestation of God), Christ's baptism, known as 'Epiphany' in the West, is celebrated. The Bible tells us, 'And it came to pass in those days, that Jesus . . . was baptized of John in the Jordan river. And straightway coming up out of the water, he saw the heavens opened, and the Spirit like a dove descending upon him, And there came a voice from heaven saying, Thou art my beloved Son, in whom I am well pleased.' The world's waters are blessed on this day, and holy water is brought home for use as needed against sickness, evil and other ills.

6 August is the feast of the **Transfiguration**. On this occasion Christ appeared to the disciples Peter, James and John in the full light of his divine glory, transfigured, on Mount Tabor in Israel. St Matthew

describes the transfiguration thus: 'Jesus taketh Peter, James, and John his brother, and bringeth them up into an high mountain apart, and was transfigured before them: and his face did shine as the sun, and his raiment was white as the light.'

On 14 September the **Elevation of the Holy Cross** celebrates the recovery from the Persians of the cross upon which Christ was crucified.

Three great feasts celebrate the life and death of the Theotokos, the God-Bearer, Mother of God, the **Holy Virgin Mary**: her **nativity** on 8 September; her **presentation in the Temple** as a young girl on 12 November; and her **dormition** on 15 August, a major feast in both Orthodox and Catholic countries. 'Dormition' means 'falling asleep', which is the term generally used for death in Orthodoxy, death being but a precursor to our reawakening to eternal life in God.

The three 'moveable feasts' whose dates are determined by Easter are:

Palm Sunday, the Sunday before Easter, marks the day Jesus entered Jerusalem riding upon a donkey colt and cheered by his supporters with cries of Hosanna! It is an occasion of joy, when fish may be eaten despite the fast. Churches are decorated inside and out with palm branches, and various figures are cleverly woven of palm leaves – crosses, stars, donkeys.

On the evening of Palm Sunday, Great Week – the period of deep mourning and strict fasting for Jesus' crucifixion – begins.

Ascension Day, forty days following Easter, marks when Jesus, after wandering the earth and appearing to many persons over a period of forty days, was taken bodily up into heaven before the eyes of the assembled company.

And finally we come to **Pentecost**, the term derived from the Greek for 'fifty'. This great holy day marks the founding of the Orthodox Church, fifty days after Christ's resurrection. On this occasion Jesus' followers were assembled together, understandably downcast and directionless after the overwhelming events of the past few months. Suddenly a sound like a wind rushed through the house, tongues of fire rested on each of them, and they were filled with the Holy Ghost (Acts 2: 1–4. See Chapter 2: The Early Church). This event is marvellous enough in itself, but it is the fact that the spirit descended upon an *assembly* of Jesus' followers, conferring *on all of them* great spiritual and intellectual powers (to speak in foreign languages, to prophesy, to heal, and to teach) that makes it especially significant in Orthodoxy. A crucial point in Orthodox theology is that the Holy Spirit descended upon many, and not on one alone or a select few: this manner of the founding of the Church explains the resolutely unstructured and democratic form – one would call it today a flat hierarchy – of the Orthodox Church throughout the world, with no single head or institutionalised body of leaders.

In addition to these twelve great holy days,
there are many more throughout the Orthodox year,
including thousands of saints' days. Every
Orthodox Christian celebrates his or her christening
in the name of a particular saint or event in Christ's
life. It was not uncommon in the past for many
Orthodox not even to know their own birthdays,
but all knew their 'name day': this was and is the
more important occasion for celebration.

Fasting: A Church Tradition

Many major holidays are preceded by a period of
fasting. The Great Fast before Easter is eight
weeks long and is particularly strict during the final
week before Easter: Great Week. There are two
weeks of fasting before 15 August, the Dormition of
the Virgin Mary, forty days before Christmas, and
the period between All Saints and the Feast of the
Apostles. Every Wednesday and Friday throughout
the year (except feast days) are fasting days, as are
the four days preceding the taking of communion.
Thus good Orthodox constantly discipline their
appetites. Fasting is a tradition – something the
Orthodox have always done. In this ancient and
conservative Church, traditions are cherished,
seldom relinquished and carefully observed.

Fasting means giving up some or even all food
and drink and other worldly pleasures for a set
period of time to purify and prepare oneself for a

serious spiritual event. As observed by the Orthodox, strict fasting means that one does not consume animals or animal products, such as meat, poultry, cheese, milk, butter and eggs; sea creatures with backbones (most fish); oil or alcohol. During the fast, one also abstains from sex and social merrymaking. The degree to which the fast is kept varies with the occasion, and there are exceptions: oil and wine are permitted on Saturdays and Sundays, fish on feast days. During most fasting periods, the Orthodox live on nuts, olives, fruit, vegetables and molluscs. Some fasting periods during the week before Easter or previous to communion require that one eat and drink nothing at all until after sundown.

Fasting is intended to turn people's attention away from physical satisfactions and towards spiritual ones. Effectively, it means that each time one sits down at table or feels hungry or thirsty, one either abstains or satisfies the appetite advisedly, according to the rules, with the approaching event and its import in mind. Thus fasting is a constant reminder of faith. Self-discipline and submission to the strictures of the fast are a sacrifice of love for Christ's Church. And when the fast is over, one delights in God's bounty with heightened joy and awareness.

Chapter 6

Church Structure

There is frequent confusion in the West about the structure of the Orthodox Church – probably because there is so little of it. People in hierarchically structured Churches often seek to ascribe to the patriarchs, such as the Ecumenical Patriarch in Constantinople, something of the role and rank of the Pope in the Catholic West, but they are not in fact comparable. Eastern Orthodoxy is essentially amorphous, with no single head or ruling body. In fact, 'The Orthodox Church' consists solely of Orthodox believers and their local bishops with their assisting clergy, united by the Holy Spirit: nothing more.

So what has kept the Orthodox together these two thousand years? Nothing but their common faith and practices. It is for this reason that Orthodox believers cling so stubbornly and undeviatingly to the Nicene Creed, to each detail of the liturgy, to the seven sacraments, to the decisions of the Seven Ecumenical Councils, and to their traditions – their numerous rituals and practices: it is these that define them as Orthodox and constitute Orthodoxy as a Church. Orthodoxy is

⊙ *Monks, priests and cantor at a chapel consecration, Greece*

thus very conservative, virtually unchanged since
Constantine's time, certainly not significantly since
the Seventh Ecumenical Council in 787. At the
same time, its non-hierarchical and localised
structure tend to make it a very democratic and
very personal Church, and very flexible in practice.

» As The Spirit Bids

How the Orthodox Church actually functions is perhaps best shown through a real-life example. A certain man joining the Orthodox Church as a monk had already been baptised as a child in a Protestant denomination. Although he recognised the necessity of being chrismated (confirmed) in the Orthodox Church (see Chapter 4: Dogma and Belief, The Seven Sacraments), he felt that to be re-baptised would be a breach of the Creed, which clearly states 'I acknowledge *One Baptism* for the remission of sins'. Besides, a second baptism would amount to a total rejection of non-Orthodox – Catholic and Protestant – baptism, implying that adherents of these Churches are not properly baptised and thus not real Christians. For his part, this candidate monk believed that Catholics and Protestants are well-meaning and Christian in spirit, if misguided. He could not accept that all these sincere and good people were not to be considered Christians at all.

His abbot, however, in the sincere conviction that there is only one true baptism, by Orthodox rite, urged the monk to reconsider and refused him the sacraments until he complied. So the monk travelled to Mount Athos to consult a holy man there about what to do. The holy man demurred, feeling it was not for him to say but for the head of the monk's own 'church', that is, his bishop. So the monk then approached the bishop responsible for his monastery. However, the bishop demurred as well, telling the monk it was for himself to decide according to his own conscience under the guidance of the Holy Spirit.

The monk, back where he had started, consulted his conscience once more and again concluded that he could not in good faith be re-baptised. Eventually the abbot, in a spirit of brotherly love and enlightened by the Holy Spirit, relented, and allowed the monk to join in the sacraments after all, without Orthodox baptism.

The head of each Orthodox flock is the bishop, who lives in his diocese, knows its people and their living conditions, and is more or less immediately accessible to all of the Orthodox living there. He is the leader, guide and arbiter in all matters within his diocese. Bishops are assisted by presbyters (priests) who have been ordained to conduct Church services. Both bishops and priests are assisted in turn, particularly during services, by deacons, who however may not conduct services or sacraments themselves. That is the Orthodox Church hierarchy in a nutshell.

The clergy – bishops, priests and deacons – are there to serve the people, their flock, Orthodox men and women. Because of the flatness of Orthodox Church hierarchy and the consequent closeness of ordinary people to the highest rank, the laity – ordinary men and women – have always had a very audible voice in Church affairs. The Church is essentially pervaded with a democratic spirit: though great respect is accorded to members of the clergy, they remain accessible and may also be readily challenged.

Bishops of important cities may enjoy a higher honorary rank as archbishop; and the bishops of cities of particular historical importance and dear to the hearts of the Orthodox – Constantinople, Alexandria, Antioch and Jerusalem – enjoy an honorary rank even higher than archbishop:

patriarch. The chief example today is the Ecumenical Patriarch in Constantinople, whose diocese in the modern city of Istanbul in Muslim Turkey is very small indeed, with at the time of writing only about fifteen hundred faithful, but whose very presence in this historically immensely important Orthodox city earns him the special reverence of Orthodox throughout the world.

The Orthodox clergy divides not only into the three hierarchical levels but also into two groupings: the priests, who are usually married and have families and live in normal houses among their parishioners; and the monks and nuns, who live celibate lives in monasteries apart from other people. Monastic communities are headed by abbots and abbesses, who are under the authority of their local bishop. Bishops, who come from the ranks of the monks, are always unmarried today, though in the early Church this was not so. A priest may marry only once in his life, before he is ordained. An unmarried woman or a widow may become a nun, an unmarried man or widower a monk. Some monks are ordained and may therefore conduct services, some not. Women may not be ordained and thus may not conduct services, though as nuns they may serve as deaconesses. Advanced study qualifies some monks and priests for the special tasks of preaching in the church and hearing confessions.

Clerics: Monks, Nuns and Priests

The division between the married and unmarried clergy serves the Orthodox community well. Monks and nuns tend to specialise in particularly spiritual matters: in the health and development of the soul. They are not mixed up in community politics and have no families to sway their thinking, exhaust their energies or undermine their impartiality. Thus monks are popular confessors. Historically, they have been closely linked to the poor and downtrodden, for whom for centuries they provided schooling, medical care and shelter, not to mention an opportunity for education and advancement. More than once they have joined forces with the common people to bring to a halt unpopular plans made over their heads by the highest and mightiest. One pivotal example was popular resistance to iconoclasm in the eighth century. Even the Emperor himself, Constantine V, his government machinery and bureaucrats, and a (non-ecumenical) Church Council proved unable to force the people, led by the monks, to accept the ban on icons.

For their part, priests understand married life, business, the raising of children, and local politics – practical matters: they serve their communities as paragons of good Christian family men. Understanding as they do the constraints, temptations and burdens of ordinary people with families and businesses, they are well positioned to advise their parishioners on dealing in a Christian manner with the problems of life in this world.

The Orthodox Church Worldwide

On a larger scale, the Orthodox are organised more or less nationally into *autocephalous* Churches – self-governing, independent units, each with its own head. There are autocephalous Churches in America, Poland, Russia, Romania, Serbia, Bulgaria, Greece, Georgia, Cyprus and the Czech Republic. The policies of these national Churches are decided at annual conferences of the bishops of each respective country. There is no international Orthodox institution as such and no one person who speaks for international Orthodoxy. There has been some discussion about selecting a spokesperson for the Orthodox Church – one possibility would be the highly regarded Ecumenical Patriarch of Constantinople – but no decision has been reached, and there is a profound mistrust within the Orthodox community of conferring even such verbal authority upon any one person, however august. International synods are held to decide questions pertinent to Orthodox belief. It is these that are definitive, since only such a council or assembly of earnest and devout Christians can – with the guidance of the Holy

Spirit as on Pentecost in AD 33 – be presumed to speak with the authority only the Holy Spirit can confer.

There are about 200–300 million Orthodox in the world, depending on whether one counts everyone baptised Orthodox as a baby or only people who actively practise their religion. In Russia there are 50–90 million Orthodox, the number constantly growing, in Romania 21 million, in North America 1–6 million. *Autonomous* Churches – Churches generally self-governing but subject in key respects to an autocephalous Church – are to be found in Finland, Sinai, Japan and Ukraine. Thus the bulk of the Orthodox live in Eastern Europe and the Balkans, and in the USA, Canada and Australia in families that originally came from these regions.

⊙ Chapter 7
Visiting an Orthodox Church

Orthodox churches offer even non-religious people refuge from the hectic world of daily life, a haven of serenity and beauty. Their intimate and subdued atmosphere is a good place to collect oneself and soothe the mind. Years ago, many Orthodox churches were always open; now this is no longer possible. Still, someone nearby often has the key to a neighbourhood church and will let visitors in: the major churches in towns are usually open at regular hours. You need do nothing to prepare for your visit but wear modest clothing (women and men) – no shorts, low necklines or bare midriffs, nothing too tight, shoulder area covered – and put yourself in a reverent, receptive frame of mind.

What Do I Do?

Upon entering an Orthodox church, the visitor must usually pause for a moment to become accustomed to the dim light. Often the walls are covered with paintings in dark colours – frescoes and icons – which create a still and cave-like atmosphere, cool in summer, sheltering in winter, always a dramatic contrast to life outside. There is the immediate sense of having entered another world, one that is full of hidden significance. The messages of this world are communicated through the objects in the church and the activities that go on there. Since these are all symbolic and ritualised, their meaning is universal and immediately accessible to all. To understand these messages, we need only open ourselves to them. Language in the usual sense of the word is not the primary medium of communication here.

⊙ Seventeenth-century chapel in the Cyclades, Greece

The interior may appear somewhat alien with its dark, sober and staring images, the glowing gold and silver, the candles, the odour of incense. If a service is going on, there is also unaccustomed music – monophonic and non-instrumental, with melodic and harmonic patterns foreign to Western ears. A priest – sometimes very elaborately and ornately clothed in silk brocade robes, bearded, magnificent, imposing, and serious to the point of severity – will be intoning prayers, often in Biblical Greek or Church Slavonic, and swinging a censer emitting smoky clouds of incense. Whether a service is in progress or not, you may well feel uncomfortable: awed, intimidated, awkward, out of place. What do you do?

This question is apt, because Orthodoxy is above all a religion of practice. Every action is significant and

⊙ *Vesper service wth priest and cantor*

meaningful. The first is the lighting of candles, which are usually directly at hand, near the church entrance. You, too, may take one or several, leaving a little money as a token sacrifice and a material gift to the Church. You then light your candle with someone or something in mind that is dear to your heart, and place it on the candle stand – often a simple tray full of sand. By performing this small action, you literally bring a little light into the world and drive out darkness: symbolically you repeat Christ's bringing the light of love and understanding into the world, eliminating the darkness of hatred and ignorance. This action, performed every time one enters a church, is a little ritual. Lighting a candle is a form of prayer. When you light a candle for someone or for the good resolution of a difficult situation, you pray in your heart for God's help. There is no need to pray in words, but the heart and mind should be well focused and open to God's guidance.

The worshipper then approaches the holy pictures, the icons: painted, deliberately two-dimensional images of saints or events in Christian history. Icons play such an important role in Orthodox worship that this book devotes a separate chapter to them. An icon may be prominently displayed on a stand in the centre of the church: this thematic icon relates to the season's particular celebrations (Christmas, Easter, the Annunciation, Pentecost, a particular saint or saints). Standing before this icon – and each icon they approach after that – worshippers make the sign of the cross over their bodies, touching in turn their forehead, heart, and right and left shoulders. They join their thumb, index and middle fingers to represent the Trinity and fold the other two fingers, the 'ring finger' and 'little finger', representing the dual human and divine nature of Christ, together into the palm of the hand. This action, like the lighting of candles, is a form of prayer: a consecration of oneself, a reverence in honour of the holy place, a recalling of Christ's crucifixion. The worshipper may then kiss the icon out of love and respect for the holy person or scene it represents. People wishing to display particular reverence may bow down before an icon, touching the floor with their fingers each time before crossing themselves. You are not obliged to do any of these things, but if you choose to view the icons more closely, you should approach them with respect and reverence.

Visitors sometimes think: so many kisses, *so many germs!* The icons are wiped regularly with alcohol to sterilise them. Then, too, wood is porous and therefore does not tend to retain bacteria. Finally, icons are credited specifically with healing powers. In any case, the Orthodox do not seem to be unusually prone to illness, so never fear. You, too, may kiss the icons if you wish, but you need not.

All of these actions – making the sign of the cross, lighting a candle this way, bowing – could be termed 'wordless prayer'. In the Orthodox way of thinking, words are often inadequate to express what is in our hearts. Nevertheless, a decided concentration is called for – what might be termed a 'collecting of one's mind and feelings in the heart' as one approaches the seat of the holy. Worshippers empty their hearts and minds of frivolity and everyday concerns to address and open themselves up to the eternal and meaningful: the holy.

The advantage of symbolic action is that its meaning is comprehensive and universal. We understand these actions even without explanation, once we leave words behind for a bit. Much of this is not really so unfamiliar. After all, even in secularised Western society, people everywhere spontaneously light candles and offer little donations – flowers or toys, for example – when they are profoundly moved: at the scene of disasters such as Ground Zero in New York City, at the site of the death of popular or dearly beloved persons, or where accidents or natural disasters have taken place. In the same natural way, we stand up when the priest enters the main church, just as we would in the presence of any person deserving of special respect. We bow our heads as a sign of reverence. Orthodoxy is practised in these terms, too.

After lighting their candles, crossing themselves and kissing the icons, worshippers may simply leave the church and go out again. This may be all that they came in for: this brief interlude of contact with the divine. If no service is in progress, you, too, may enjoy such an interlude, or talk quietly with a friend or walk about the church.

As long as you are dressed modestly, you should not hesitate to come in, even if a service is in progress. If your apparel and behaviour proclaim your respect and goodwill, you may be sure that you are very welcome. People are pleased that you are there and take an interest in the religion so dear to their hearts. You need not do anything but behave respectfully, and you can leave again whenever there is a lull in the proceedings. (This is not all right for the Orthodox, but it is all right for you. People will understand.) Orthodox services, if you do not know what is going on, can seem very long.

You may stand to the side or at the back, or take a seat anywhere but on the ornate bishop's throne on your right near the iconostasis (see opposite), where no one sits but the bishop himself. In some countries, women usually sit together on one side of the church, men on the other, but it is not uncommon for visitors to switch sides, and no one will mind if you sit down with your husband, wife, partner or friend.

Certain body language is considered respectful and appropriate in Orthodox churches. You should either stand upright on both feet, your hands at your sides or clasped before you, or sit facing forward, feet on the floor, hands in your lap. You should not cross your legs at the knee, which is considered too worldly and casual a posture, clasp your hands behind your back, or stretch out your legs before you.

If a service is going on, the priest will enter the main part of the church, where you are sitting, from time to time. When he does it is appropriate to stand up. If he swings his censer in your direction, do not be alarmed! He is blessing you. You may acknowledge his kindly goodwill by bowing your head toward him.

That is all you need to do, so now you can just relax, enjoy yourself, and turn your attention to

your usually quite spectacular, quite wonderful
surroundings.

What Am I Looking At?

As you look around, your attention will surely be
drawn first to the striking screen of icons, broken
by two or three doors. This *iconostasis* divides the
eastern part of the church, the sanctuary, with the
altar, from the western part, where you sit. At the
centre is the *holy gate*, a two-leafed portal often
portraying the Archangel Gabriel announcing to the
Virgin Mary that God has chosen her to bear His
Son (see Chapter 1: Jesus' Life). Immediately to the
right of the holy gate, as you face the iconostasis, is
Jesus Christ; to the left is his mother, the Virgin

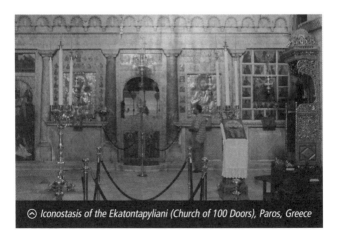

⊙ *Iconostasis of the Ekatontapyliani (Church of 100 Doors), Paros, Greece*

Mary. To the right of Jesus is the icon of the saint
or event from which that particular church takes its
name. To the left of the icon of the Virgin is another
door, upon which the Archangel Michael usually
appears, guarding the entrance to the sanctuary
with his sword. There is almost always an icon of
St John the Baptist somewhere on the iconostasis
or near it, wearing the rough tunic of skins that
identifies him as a desert-dweller. He is usually
depicted with wings, since he served as a
messenger (in Greek: *angelos*) sent to prepare for
the coming of Christ. Along the top of the
iconostasis, a series of icons shows events in the
life of Christ and His mother: for example, His birth,
baptism, transfiguration on Mount Tabor, healing of
the sick, harrowing before Pontius Pilate,
crucifixion and resurrection. Atop the iconostasis is
Christ crucified on the cross with dragons below
symbolising the underworld of evil defeated. Above
Christ's head are the letters 'INBI', the Greek
equivalent of the Latin 'INRI', standing for 'Jesus of
Nazareth, King of the Jews', which the Roman
authorities wrote on the cross in Latin, Greek and
Hebrew to mock Jesus when they crucified Him.

There will be many more icons in the church as
well, picturing some of the thousands of saints
revered by Orthodox worshippers, or depicting
famous scenes from the saints' lives or other
religiously significant events. Right up to the second
half of the twentieth century, many people in

Orthodox areas could not read: pictures were the medium that conveyed to them the events related in the scripture. Even today, with almost universal literacy, pictures have a unique impact: they communicate immediately and memorably messages that are none the less profound for being non-verbal. Holy persons are indicated with a halo, a golden circle of light, around their heads. Within Christ's halo we see the outlines of the cross and within them the Greek O Ω N, which means 'The One Who Is' – as God designated Himself (Exodus 3: 14). Very holy people have been seen actually to emit this light or aura: it is the light of the divine shining forth from within them.

Strung beneath some icons you may see a row of small, flat, oblong pieces of gold or silver stamped with an arm, a leg, eyes, the figure of a woman or man, a baby, a foot, a hand, a house, a horse, a ship, a heart, etc. These are votives: the offerings of grateful worshippers for prayers granted through the intercession of the saint before whose icon they have prayed, or by Christ Himself. If sets of eyes predominate, for instance, this means that people credit that saint with particular assistance with diseases of the eyes. Sometimes the offerings are more than simple votives – gold earrings or even diamond necklaces from the worldly great and powerful. Famous icons, such as the Virgin of Tinos, may be wholly encrusted with such offerings, so that the icon itself can scarcely be seen. To the frustration of art lovers, the faithful, in gratitude, sometimes also cover icons with silver, leaving only the face and a hand revealed.

Before each icon hangs an ornate little oil lamp that lights up the icon and attests to the attention of the faithful, who keep it burning within the dim church day and night in honour of the saint.

Orthodox churches are built more or less on an east–west axis, with the sanctuary toward the east and the entrance doors in the west. The iconostasis thus always faces toward the west. This position in relation to the sun is important to Orthodox worship: it harmonises with the texts of the morning and evening services, which refer to the rising and setting sun, the beginning and ending of each day – the natural rhythm that governs all of our lives.

The Sanctuary

The sanctuary is sequestered behind the iconostasis. It is a holy place, reserved for certain persons only. Non-Orthodox visitors should never enter the sanctuary – not even when the church is empty. Nor should they peer into it through the holy gate in the centre of the iconostasis, or even stand on the little central stone step before it. If no service is going on, you may look into the sanctuary through the door at the left of the iconostasis with the image of St Michael the archangel, identifiable by his wings, armour and sword.

⊙ *Altar at Church of the Archangel Michael, Paros*

Within the sanctuary you will see two 'tables': the larger one in the middle is the altar, the centre of church liturgical practice, covered with cloth. Either within the altar, embedded within the stonework itself, or in a special cloth brought along to the service and laid atop the altar, is a relic – a piece of a holy object or a remainder of a holy person – which lends its holiness to the altar. To the Orthodox way of thinking, there is no clear division between the material world and the spiritual, non-material world. Things seen and unseen are equally real. Thus a saint's bone ensures the very presence of the saint himself in the church – in body and in spirit.

Atop the altar one often sees a book, the Gospel used in services and consisting of excerpts from the New Testament of the Bible, usually large and very ornately encased in silver and jewels. A book of 'offices' contains the evening, morning and other services. On the altar stand a cross, candles, which burn throughout a service, and the 'tabernacle', an ornate coffer containing the consecrated bread and wine, the body and blood of Christ. These are always at hand in case of emergency: if someone becomes seriously ill, the priest will offer them communion with this bread and wine in the hope of their recovery or to prepare them for death.

Behind the altar stand poles bearing disks with images of six-winged angels – the seraphim – and a cross with the body of Christ crucified.

To the left of the altar, a small table or recess in the wall holds other objects used in Orthodox worship: the paten, a small tray upon which the communion bread is placed; the chalice for the communion wine; the small knife, the 'lance', for cutting the communion bread; the spoon with which the Eucharist is given to worshippers; and cloth covers for the paten and chalice. The diptych may be here as well – a two-leafed tablet with the names of persons particularly important to the community of the faithful.

In very old churches, rows of seats are set into the curve of the apse. It was here that the assembled clergy used to sit, with the bishop at the centre in a special throne-like seat. These are seldom used today: usually icons or other holy objects are placed on them.

There may also be a kind of basin in the sanctuary for the washing of holy objects: the water is thus channelled directly into the earth itself, which as God's own creation is holy.

The Body of the Church

Outside the sanctuary, in the main body of the church, other objects of interest will catch your eye. To the right front is a high-backed, especially ornate seat, a throne, where the bishop sits when he attends a service in the church and which is reserved for him alone at all times. In larger churches, there may be a raised pulpit, approached by a series of steps, for preaching. A revolving lectern toward the side or the back of the church holds the texts for the cantors, specially trained singers who chant the responses to the priest during services. The back and side walls are usually lined with a unique kind of wooden seat especially designed for worship. These are practical for short periods of sitting or repeated standing and sitting; they fold up so that one can stand within, resting one's arms on the armrests. Orthodox often stand throughout services, as is indeed recommended for all but the elderly or weak.

In large or particularly important churches there may be a permanent font for baptisms – sometimes, in very ancient churches, built into the floor in the shape of a cross. You may also see in the church a small and very ornate case containing a relic – a bone, perhaps, of a holy person. In older churches there may also be a *gynekeion* – a gallery along the sides or back of the church where women sometimes stood to be apart from the congregation as a whole.

What Is Going On?

About Church Services

Purpose and Method

The purpose of Orthodox services is to worship God – not to analyse Him or to speculate about His actions or to raise moral issues. Every aspect of each service is an attempt to use our limited human skills to produce a form of worship that is worthy of God. The sober and spiritually expressive icons, the precious and ornately carved gold and silver, the constant chanting of the service texts in intricate, prescribed and shifting musical patterns, the complex and ancient order of the services themselves, the candles, the gleaming, polished brass candle stands, the priest's brocaded vestments, the richly decorated chalices and incense burners, the sweet-smelling, precious incense in the silver censer: all is intended to be beautiful, dignified, serious and reverent – and to be intensely experienced both spiritually and physically. Each object and every gesture has a spiritual purpose and meaning. They are meant to appeal to the eyes, the ears, the nose, and the mouth as well as to the spirit, the mind and the feelings: to the whole person. The movements and gestures of the people – bowing, crossing oneself, kissing the icons, kneeling, kissing the hand of the priest in respect for his office – all are expressions of worship. Orthodox worship is a wholly spiritual and wholly physical experience.

Priestly Apparel

The clothes the priest wears are just one example of the detailed symbolism of Orthodox worship. The priest is the instrument of Christ: it is his duty to

⊙ *Priest celebrating the sacrament of holy unction*

perform the sacraments for the benefit of the people. He – and in Orthodoxy all priests are men – usually knows each of his parishioners by name and serves as their personal guide and support in worship. His most important role is to perform the liturgy, in which the bloodless sacrifice – the Eucharist (from the Greek for 'thanksgiving') – is offered and in which the community of the faithful participate.

The unique and special nature of his office is reflected in his clothing, of which each item is meaningful and is donned with reverence and prayer. His long-sleeved tunic reaches to the ground. Over the tunic hangs the stole, a strip of cloth that encircles the neck and hangs to the hem of the tunic. The stole symbolises priestly power and is worn whenever the priest is exercising that power. Yoke-like, it signifies the burden of his office. The girdle around the priest's waist holds the stole in place. Special cuffs encircle his wrists to enable freedom of movement. The *epigonation*, a stiff, diamond-shaped piece of reinforced cloth, hangs from the girdle to the knee. It recalls the cloth with which Christ washed the feet of his disciples, and as such the priest's commitment to serve others in humility; and it signifies, too, the sword of the spirit, with which the priest is armed. Finally, covering all of these, is the chasuble, a long cape, very ornate and richly embroidered, recalling in its cloak-like form the wandering of the Apostles and reminding the priest that he is a sojourner in this world.

The act of putting on all of these ritual items of clothing prepares the priest spiritually for the holy offices he will perform. Bit by bit, as he dons each article, the priest is transformed from a private man – usually married and with a family – into a man of God: fully clothed, he emerges prepared for his holy work as 'the salt of the earth' and 'the light of the world'.

Language
Services are held in the language of the country or of the majority of the congregation. Orthodox services in Germany, for instance, are conducted either in German or in the language of the congregation's home country. The point is that everybody should understand. For this reason translators have played an important role in Church history and have even been sainted, as were Cyril and Methodios, brothers

who translated the Greek service into Slavonic, thus bringing the Christian message and Christian worship to millions of people in Eastern Europe. In Greece, services are in *koine*, the form of everyday Greek spoken during the late Classical and Byzantine periods and the root of modern Greek. Most Orthodox understand church language with varying degrees of success. All can follow the familiar services, and many know them by heart.

Formalism

Despite the extravagant surroundings and elaborate ritual, Orthodox services may appear nonchalant to many Western visitors, with children moving freely about the church and people coming and going and talking and – seemingly randomly – coming forward to perform various actions. This is all very unlike the formality of Western services, with people sitting quietly in rows and listening attentively. It is important to bear in mind, however, that Orthodox worshippers – however casual they may appear – are constantly and intensely aware of being in the presence of a holy proceeding. True, children are granted great freedom: they are supposed to love their church and to love being there – to feel at home and unconstrained. Adults are supposed to come on time to services and stay until they end. But maybe they cannot. In such cases it is better that they at least stop by and light a candle, or come late if they are delayed, or stay as long as they can

if they must leave. People are supposed to be quiet
in church and to concentrate on the service, but
most Orthodox know the services backwards and
forwards, are aware of it constantly in their hearts,
certainly, and sometimes cannot resist a remark to a
neighbour.

Liturgical Dialogue

Orthodox services are actually a dialogue between
the priest and congregation, represented by the
cantors, who are grouped around the lighted,
revolving lectern, usually nowadays superfluously
equipped with a microphone. Now that
congregations are more literate and educated than
they have been in the past, they often wish to play a
more active role in services, so they respond to the
priest themselves, chanting along with the cantors,
as was actually the original practice in the early
Church. And now that women play a more active role
in society, they too have been welcomed into this
previously male role. Except for the Lord's Prayer, the
Creed and the sermon (if there is one), the entire
service is sung or chanted by both the priest and the
cantors; no musical instruments are permitted.

The Sermon

Notably abbreviated in Orthodox services compared
to services in Western churches, or absent
altogether, is the sermon. When a sermon is
preached at all, it is usually a brief and

straightforward explanation of what the Gospel reading means on a quite simple level, or a historical summary, for instance, of a saint's life. There is no conjecture, speculation or departure into the realm of the abstract or intellectual, nor is there any particular moralising. The idea is that the scripture is clear and cannot be improved upon, that if you love God and your neighbour and act accordingly, you cannot go wrong. There is no need to split hairs or stir up debate. If you cannot see how to behave in a Christian manner in a given situation, you can always turn to a monk or priest for guidance.

Regular Services
In major churches, the morning service (matins) and the evening service (vespers) are held every day. The liturgy (mass) is celebrated on Sundays and feast days, immediately after matins. It is this combining of these two morning services – and sometimes other ones as well, such as the blessing of bread, oil and wine, or a memorial service for someone deceased – that leads people to think Orthodox services very long. Actually, the liturgy takes only about an hour, matins and vespers about 30 to 45 minutes. Still, it is true that when it comes to worship the Orthodox take their time. Prayer cannot be rushed or initiated instantaneously: it is a serious undertaking that calls for adequate preparation and ample time.

The Liturgy

The liturgy usually begins around 8:15 in the morning, following immediately upon the heels of matins, which has begun at about 7.00. Thus when most worshippers arrive, they enter immediately into an atmosphere of worship. 'Liturgy' means 'common work or endeavour' in Greek, and this service is in fact a joint effort by everyone present to praise God. The whole liturgy centres upon the bloodless sacrifice or holy meal of bread and wine that worshippers partake of, as Jesus asked them to do, in remembrance of Him: 'And he took bread, and gave thanks, and brake it, and gave unto them, saying, This is my body which is given for you: this do in remembrance of me. Likewise also the cup after supper, saying, This cup is the new testament in my blood, which is shed for you.' (Luke 22: 19–20)

The service begins with the words 'Blessed be the kingdom of the Father, and of the Son, and of the Holy Spirit, now and forever and from all ages to all ages'. This is followed by a series of short prayers for all sorts of things: the welfare of the town, an angel to guard one's body and soul, the release of captives, the peace of the world, favourable weather, travellers, the sick, forgiveness of sins, deliverance from affliction, wrath, danger and need, and a death that is painless, blameless and peaceful. As the service proceeds, you may see people handing in lists of names through the door at the left of the iconostasis: the priest will pray for these persons during the service, either aloud or to himself. People may also submit loaves of bread as offerings for the use of the church.

After certain preparations, and saying 'Wisdom! Stand up!' the priest enters the main part of the church bearing the Gospel aloft and proceeds with it around the church. People stand, bow their heads in respect for the word of God, and cross themselves before the Holy Scripture. Two readings from the Bible follow: one from the letters of SS Paul, John, James, Peter or Jude, or during Eastertide from the Acts of the Apostles, read by one of the cantors or another qualified person, the other from one of the four Gospels – SS Matthew, Mark, Luke or John – read by the priest.

At times throughout the service the priest swings a vessel of burning incense, blessing the icons and the people and filling the church with a pleasing scent. People bow their heads in respect as the priest passes, swinging the incense in their direction.

Elaborate preparations are made – mostly behind the iconostasis – for the climax of the service, the Eucharist, the bloodless sacrifice, the holy gifts of bread and wine, Christ's body and blood. When these have been prepared and blessed, the cantors, on behalf of the people, sing the following Cherubic hymn, preparing the congregation for the sacrifice to come.

*Let us who mystically represent the
Cherubim and chant the thrice-holy hymn to
the Life-giving Trinity, put away all worldly
care so that we may receive the King of all.*

This hymn is interrupted by the entrance of the
priest into the main body of the church, bearing the
holy gifts among the assembled people, who rise,
bow and cross themselves as they did before the
Gospel.

The Nicene Creed (see Chapter 4: Dogma and
Belief) is then recited in its original form either by
an individual or by the entire congregation.

The priest then withdraws behind the
iconostasis once more and calls upon the Holy Spirit
to descend upon the bread and wine, so that Christ
may be really present in them, though in a manner
we cannot comprehend. This is the high point of
the service, when the Holy Spirit is perceived to be
actually present within the church and amongst the
worshippers: it is a moment of profound
concentration and prayer. It is customary in some
parishes for the entire congregation to kneel.

After a series of brief prayers, the Lord's Prayer
(see Chapter 1: Jesus' Life) is spoken either by an
individual or by the congregation in unison.

Then Orthodox Christians who wish to take part
in communion, and have prepared themselves with
confession, fasting and prayer, come forward. They
are given the Eucharist, the body and blood of

Christ present in the bread immersed in wine, on a spoon from a common chalice.

The priest then consumes the remainder of the Eucharist, rinses the chalice with water, which he drinks, wipes out the chalice with a special cloth and later washes the cloth in the special basin for this purpose in the sanctuary, so that any trace of Christ's body and blood descends directly into God's earth.

The service ends not long after this climax, and everyone presses forward, greets and is greeted by the priest, and is given a piece of blessed bread to eat. Non-Orthodox visitors may partake of this *antidoron*, but not of the Eucharist, which is reserved for Orthodox communicants.

The Evening Service: Vespers

A service that non-Orthodox visitors may find particularly enjoyable and accessible is vespers, which takes place in a town's main church every day at around sunset. It lasts about half an hour. The time for vespers changes throughout the year with the hour of sunset. In mid-summer it is usually at around 7:00 p.m., but it may take place at any time in the late afternoon or early evening. The point of this service is to give thanks for the day that is past and to anticipate the day to come. Since the liturgical day begins at sunset, the readings take up the saint or event to be celebrated the following day. The service begins with Psalm 103 (104 in the Western numbering system) (see Chapter 4: Dogma and Belief), which is read every day of the year except during the week after Easter and the day of Christ's crucifixion, the Friday immediately before Easter known as Great (Good) Friday. This psalm is a long hymn of praise to God as He reveals himself in nature. In Orthodox terms, destruction of the natural world, God's creation, is a desecration, and the Orthodox Church has been active in introducing sounder ecological practices in monastic farming and elsewhere ever since the horrors of environmental destruction were first recognised.

A striking hymn in the vesper service is the *phos ilaron*, the 'hymn of joyous light', which is spoken, sung or chanted. This hymn is probably the oldest in the Church, dating apparently from the second century AD. The hymn's imagery weaves together the light of the sun and the light of the Son, Christ Himself, who is 'light of light', as the Creed proclaims. This hymn must have had very special significance to early converts, many of whom, like Constantine the Great, were sun-worshippers before they became Christians and were sensitive to the wonder of light. For us today, too, this hymn is especially moving in Orthodox churches at sunset, when the mellow golden sunlight of early evening shines through the church's western doors onto the iconostasis and the icon of Christ Himself, and we can thank God for the gift of another day of our lives. It goes like this:

> *O joyful light of holy glory of the undying, heavenly, holy, blessed Father, O Jesus Christ.*

> *Having come to the setting of the sun and beholding the evening light, we raise our hymn to Father, Son and Holy Spirit: God.*

> *For it was ever meet and right to voice the hymn of praise:*

> *O Son of God, Wellspring of Life, all the world glorifies you.*

Other Services

There are numerous other services to meet all sorts of human spiritual needs – blessings at the start of each new month; blessing of the basic foods of oil, wine and bread; prayers for succour in time of trouble or sickness; prayers for rain; prayers of thanks; prayers of supplication; prayers for women who have given birth; services in memory of the dead (on the third, ninth and fortieth days following the death, quarterly, and on the anniversary of the death); and many others. The Orthodox want their religion to permeate and grace all of their lives, including their business lives and home lives. Thus their religion is not confined to churches: they have the priest come to bless their houses, their cars, their shops, their fishing boats, their animals, their fields, the sea and the land.

Chapter 8

Icons

Icons are so essential to Orthodox worship that
they merit a chapter of their own. They are found
not only in great numbers in churches but in every
Orthodox home, on ships, in automobiles, buses,
workshops, shops – everywhere the Orthodox lead
their lives. Icons are neither merely decorative nor
strictly instructional: they are aids to worship, to
Christian prayer and meditation, and to absorption
of the Christian message. They are holy pictures.
What the Orthodox experience through icons is the
presence of the Holy Spirit as revealed through the
depicted personages or scenes. They *love* the icons
for conveying this presence, which is why they kiss
them. Icons have been called 'windows to the soul'
and 'windows to eternity': indeed, the icon is not
an end in itself but a door to a spiritual dimension.

Western art – even Western religious art – does
not prepare us for this kind of encounter or this kind
of subject matter. People seeing icons for the first
time – even people well versed in art generally –
often find it hard to 'connect' with icons. They feel
that icons simply do not convey anything much, that
– two-dimensional as they are – they are primitive in

⊙ *The Resurrection of the Dead. Christ raising Adam, with prophets and saints*

terms of technique and cold or remote in expression.
This may be partly because of confusion about their
subject matter: it is misleading to think of icons
simply as portraits of saints or renderings of biblical
events. The icon's true subject matter lies in another
dimension entirely. Icon-painting techniques are
used advisedly, to convey content not usually
attempted in art: specifically religious, spiritual
content. As Rubens, for instance, conveyed the
richness of the flesh, or as van Gogh or Seurat
conveyed the play of light, or as Rembrandt conveyed
people's characters, so great icons convey the spirit
of holiness.

Anyone can learn to perceive the icons' message.
It is merely a matter of practice – of putting aside
one's preconceptions about what art should be and
looking at the icons with an open mind. With time,
the icons' message will communicate itself to
anyone who is receptive, as all worthwhile art does.
The effort has its rewards: after all, we did not
understand the Old Masters either when we first
saw them as children, but with experience and
maturity we now derive great satisfaction from
them. We must exercise ourselves in icon-viewing
if we want to benefit from icons.

The personage or scene in the icon serves as the
medium for this message and particularises it; but the
subject must not be allowed to obscure the
fundamental, fourth-dimensional message. Three-
dimensional art inevitably stresses the physical world,

which is why there is no sculpture in Orthodox churches. The absence of shading and perspective in icons is often mistakenly attributed to the painter's lack of technical skill. But the two-dimensional technique is used on purpose to help us move beyond the physical subject matter – the wooden icon with human subjects reproduced in paint – to the actual content beyond it. Thus the hallmark of icon technique is restraint. The true subject matter is so important, so significant, that it would be impossible to portray it: it can only be suggested.

A great icon actually portrays the *Logos* – God's very message or meaning or purpose or essence: this is the real subject matter. It is this subject that makes icons into aids to worship, to Christian prayer and meditation, to absorption of the Christian message and achievement of a spiritual state. This is a very tall order for the artist, who must be not only a skilled craftsperson but also an individual of considerable spiritual insight and depth. Certainly not all icon painters are up to this great task, and so not all icons fully 'succeed'. Nevertheless, all icons – sharing, as they do, a prescribed and similar style and content – convey at least an echo, however faint, of this ambitious goal, so that God's grace is present in all of them, and all are holy.

To approach this difficult and elusive subject, serious icon painters – often monks or nuns – will fast and pray before beginning to paint, attempting to achieve insight into the particular spiritual nature of the great personality they are attempting to portray. When they feel they comprehend this, they use their skill as painters to imbue their subject with it. And if they succeed, you and I can benefit from this communication and, as observers, perceive the saint's holiness ourselves. Having put aside their own egos to identify with the saint, icon painters usually consider the Holy Spirit to be the actual artist, and for this reason do not sign the icon but choose to remain anonymous.

Some icons succeed so well in their purpose that one could claim without exaggeration that to understand these icons is to encounter the *Logos* itself – the very message of God – and thus to comprehend the essence of Christian belief. Two prime examples would be the icon of Christ in St Catherine's monastery on Mount Sinai and the mosaic Deisis of Christ, the Virgin Mary and St John the Baptist in the upper gallery of St Sophia in Istanbul. Fortunately, there are thousands of great icons everywhere in the world to open our souls to this experience.

Icon painters must adhere to strict parameters in their work. Guided by other icons, they know something of what the saint looked like, and they faithfully reproduce the essentials of his or her features. Not just anyone is portrayed, but a specific human being who actually lived and had a recognisable face: with a little experience one can

identify the saints from their faces alone. Orthodox
icon painters are not permitted to deviate from
these features, because then it would no longer be
the saint who is portrayed but someone else, or a
figment of the artist's imagination. To the extent
that the icon is a picture of someone, it is a picture
of that person *transfigured* with holiness,
somewhat as Christ was transfigured when He
revealed himself to His disciples Peter, James and
John on Mount Tabor.

⊙ An icon painter at work

Objects that are traditionally associated with the
saint may be introduced as well, and these also
help the worshipper to identify the saint.

St Catherine will be shown with the wheel on
which she was tortured, St John the Baptist
wearing the skins of wild animals, St Nicholas in
the robes of a bishop, and so on. The golden halo
about the saint's head represents the light of
holiness that emanated from the person – his or her
perceptible aura of light.

Particularly during the eighth and ninth centuries,
there was prolonged and bitter controversy over the
use of icons in Orthodox worship. Icons painted
before that time are rare not only because of their
age but because iconoclasts destroyed them *en
masse*. Even today feelings run high over the uses of
images in worship. Some visitors to Orthodox
churches may be put off by the attention the
Orthodox pay to icons, seeing in this idolatry or
superstition. The devout Orthodox, for their part, love
the presence of holiness in their icons. It is this that
they reverence when they light a candle or cross
themselves before an icon; it is their love for the holy
person that they express with a kiss.

A modern Greek icon-painter (quoted by Patricia
Storace in her book *Dinner with Persephone*)
described his feelings about icons in the following
rather polemical but nevertheless instructive terms:

> '. . . *our pictures, the pictures in the Byzantine
> tradition, are dogmatismena [imbued with
> dogma], they are incarnations of theology,
> they are God's fingerprints. And they are the*

legacy of the greatest empire the world has known, the Byzantine Empire, which fixed its ambition on the supernatural and the eternal. As I do when I paint. I decorporealize, I dematerialize the saint; the painting becomes prayer, the saint's body not an earthly body but a heavenly one . . . The classical Greeks expressed perfect earthly beauty, and we complete them by expressing perfect divine beauty . . . Western [religious] painting . . . is nothing more than painted opera, and has no relation to either the letter or the spirit of the gospel, the gospel which is so simple that it confounds the labyrinths of the philosophers. Even our holy city is bodiless . . . our leader . . . is the patriarch of Constantinople. And you will say, but there is no Constantinople; this patriarch lives in Istanbul. But our Constantinople, like an angel, is a bodiless city, the leading city of a bodiless angelic empire . . . [In our art] we make sacraments. Ours is true Christian art, yours is nothing but decorated egotism . . . Byzantine architecture is on a human scale, with the exception of Agia Sophia, God surrounds man, God sees man, whether he wills it or not . . . .'

Chapter 9

Eastern and Western Christianity

Why the Christian World Split

Why is there today an Eastern Orthodox Church and
a Western Church made up of Catholics and
Protestants? Why did we not all just stay Christians,
as we were for a thousand years? One gets a
picture from the history books that quite suddenly,
in 1054, there was one big quarrel over the abstruse
Latin word *filioque*, on account of which, in a fit of
pique, as it were, East went east and West went
west. But there is much more to it than that. First,
to thoughtful Christians, the *filioque* issue is not
abstruse at all, since the balance within the Trinity,
the Christian concept of God, hangs on this point.
But aside from theology, the pressures leading up to
the split had in fact been building for many
centuries: in the mid-eleventh century they finally
burst forth. Let us look at a few of the notable steps
on the long road to schism.

The first step was doubtless Constantine's
decision in 324 to establish a 'second Rome',
Constantinople (Istanbul today), on the site of the
little town of Byzantium on the Bosporus. This

decision may well have saved the Roman Empire from collapse by moving the centre of power to a safer location than the Italian peninsula, far from the increasingly devastating incursions of the barbarians; but it also created two poles where there had been only one:

⊘ *The double-headed eagle, emblem of the Byzantine Empire*

the city of Rome. Appropriately, the symbol of the Byzantine Empire, as historians came to call the Eastern Roman Empire, was the double-headed eagle, which appears in church art today throughout the former Byzantine world. When the Emperor Constantine built Constantinople as his capital city and moved his court and the bulk of the Roman leadership there, the split of the Roman Empire into East and West was sealed. The East looked towards newly built, glittering, vigorous Constantinople, while the West looked towards venerable, gorgeous, 'eternal' but teetering Rome. Constantinople was formally inaugurated in 330.

The barbarian invasions from the third to the eighth century, and the rise of Islam in the seventh, further divided East from West. Starting in the seventh century, Saracen (Arab) corsairs cruised the Mediterranean, raiding the coasts and islands for booty and slaves, sacking towns and villages pretty much at will, disrupting or cutting off communications, and shaking the settled, unified, 'civilised' world of that day to its very foundations. The Mediterranean islands were gradually depopulated. Travel and trade throughout the empire – once frequent, flourishing and relatively safe – deteriorated and became risky and uncertain. Church dignitaries, like everyone else, travelled reluctantly, so that truly ecumenical councils, with representatives from all over the empire, ceased to be held after the eighth century. People stayed at home in the East or in the West. This situation lasted for centuries, until the Italian city-states – most notably Venice – brought the pirates to heel and made trade possible once more. But during the long centuries of separation, the Latin West and the Greek East more or less went their own ways, developing their own cultures and religious practices, which gradually came to differ significantly from one another. Put very broadly, the

Western Church tended to scholasticism – the intellect, analysis and dispute; the East to mysticism – the spirit, inspiration and synthesis.

The linguistic split between the Latin-speakers of the West and the Greek-speakers of the East expressed and cemented this division at one and the same time. At the time of Christ, the language of the Roman bureaucracy and army was Latin: the language of culture and civilised society was Greek. From about the third century BC to the fifth century AD, people in urban, educated and cultured circles throughout the empire spoke both languages. The vernacular in the West was Latin, in the East, Greek; and people in rural areas spoke hundreds of other languages and dialects as well. Roman coins expressed this cosmopolitanism, being sometimes minted in both Greek and Latin. But in the early seventh century, with Rome sacked, ruined, and depopulated, the Byzantine Emperor Heraclius changed the official language of the government from Latin to Greek. Constantinople grew into a great metropolis with eventually nearly a million inhabitants, while Rome declined into ruin with a population numbered in hundreds. Instead of two international languages spoken throughout the empire, Greek disappeared in the West, as Latin did in the East.

In the ninth century, in a final desperate move to close the yawning rift in the civilised world, Charlemagne and the Byzantine Empress Irene contemplated marriage. Their union might have united the world once more, at least for a time; but in the event it was not to be, and the hope for a single empire perished forever. In any case, ninth-century Westerners would no doubt have been horrified at having a wily, wilful queen from the duplicitous, to them heretical, inscrutable East, and the Byzantines, for their part, would have been shocked at having illiterate Charlemagne – to them an uncultured, heretical boor – as king.

Various differences in practice arose. The Eastern Church used leavened bread for the Eucharist, the Western Church unleavened. Priests in the Eastern Church were bearded. Priests in the Western Church were celibate; in the Eastern Church priests married (previous to ordination). Then there was the *filioque* – Latin for 'and the son' – which began to appear in the section of the Creed pertaining to the Holy Spirit – sometime during the sixth century.

> *'I believe . . . in the Holy Spirit, the Lord, the Giver of Life, Who proceedeth from the Father* [and the son], *Who with the Father and the Son is worshipped and glorified.'*

In Western Europe, many Christians welcomed the *filioque* as confirming the divine nature of Christ and silencing the Arian heretics who claimed that Jesus was purely human in nature. For six hundred years, generally worsening communications between East and West, along with a desire on all sides not to rock the Christian boat, permitted this along with other discrepancies at the heart of Christian dogma to be tolerated or diplomatically overlooked.

But with the rising power of the Pope, the *filioque* became an issue – not solely for doctrinal reasons but because of the papal authority the change implied. The Creed had been put into final form and confirmed by the Council of Constantinople in 381. Changes had been expressly prohibited at two Nicaean councils and the councils at Ephesus and Chalcedon. What aroused animosity in the East was not only the doctrinal change but the assumption of authority by a single bishop, the Bishop of Rome, in instituting a change not confirmed by an Ecumenical Council recognised by the Universal Church. (The addition was much disputed in the West as well, where several popes also rejected the *filioque*: still, in the end it carried the day there.)

In 1054, disputes among popes, cardinals, patriarchs and emperors brought all of these issues out of the dusk of oversight, where they had been kept for centuries by peace- and unity-loving Christians everywhere, into the glare of scrutiny. Ineptitude and stubbornness on both sides prevented discussion and excluded compromise.

The Byzantines failed to support the papalists in their struggle against the Normans in Sicily. With papal support, the victorious Normans then forced Latin traditions on the Greek churches there. The patriarch in Constantinople retaliated by forcing Latin parishes in Constantinople to adopt Greek church customs. Furious letters, with deprecating terms of address, were exchanged, further muddled by poor translation. Finally, the Pope, Leo IX, dispatched particularly undiplomatic and uncompromising persons as legates to Constantinople. Following a series of diplomatic *faux pas* and misunderstandings, the legates then took it upon themselves to place a Bull (edict) of Excommunication against the Byzantine patriarch Cerularius, citing a series of spurious transgressions, upon the high altar of St Sophia. The Byzantines responded by burning the Bull and anathematising the legates.

In fact, both excommunications were directed at individuals and not at the two respective Churches; yet the effect was the same – schism.

Although the date 1054 persists in the minds of students of Church history everywhere as marking the division between East and West, at the time most people were simply not aware of it. Communications, as we have seen, were physically and linguistically poor. And in the eleventh century, in any case, neither ordinary Westerners nor ordinary Easterners could have conceived of there being two legitimate Christian Churches. The idea persisted in the minds of Christians everywhere that there was, as there always had been, one God, one civilised world, and one Church. For a hundred and fifty years, the 'schism' was simply ignored by ordinary Christians everywhere, who carried on with their faith as usual and accepted all other Christians as communicants, *filioque* or no.

The East–West division actually came to be sealed in 1204, when an army of Venetian-led Franks en route to Jerusalem – Crusaders on their way to free the Holy Land from the Infidel – took a detour to the fabulously wealthy city of Constantinople and sacked it. They ripped its treasures from walls and pillars, committed outrages such as orgies in St Sophia, and in a rampage of vandalism and debauchery destroyed every sort of private, public and ecclesiastical property. Specimens of this pillage – pillars, icons, the famous bronze horses – are to be seen to this day adorning the Church of St Mark's in Venice. The destruction was immense, gratuitous, and particularly painful to the Orthodox for having been committed by fellow-Christians. It set the minds of the Byzantines, and their successor Greeks, against the Western Church for centuries to come. An apology for this enormity was finally made to Orthodox leaders in Athens in 2001 by Pope John Paul II.

Neither the city of Constantinople nor the Byzantine/Roman Empire ever really recovered from

⊙ *The Crusader sack of Constantinople, 1204. Painting by Palma Le Jeune*

this terrible blow. Thus weakened, they proved
unable to withstand the assaults of the steadily
advancing Ottoman Turks over the course of the
thirteenth, fourteenth, and fifteenth centuries.
Finally, during the night of 29 May 1453, 1,123
years after its founding, the glorious city fell. The
emperor threw himself into the fray and went down
fighting. His body was never recovered. The Greek
Orthodox Church entered into centuries of
subjection to Turkish rule that ended only with the
Greek War of Independence in 1821. (A tiny Greek
minority of some fifteen hundred souls still lives in
Istanbul under the shadow of the threat of violence,

and the Patriarch of Constantinople continues to occupy the patriarchal residence there.) But meanwhile Orthodoxy had spread beyond the reach of any single invader – throughout the Balkans and the Slavic countries and, most important, to Russia's vastnesses, where it has in our time enjoyed a robust revival following the break-up of the Soviet Union.

Differences among the Christian Churches

In North America and Western Europe, Catholicism and Protestantism are the dominant forms of Christianity; in Greece, Russia, parts of Eastern Europe and the Balkans, Orthodoxy is. The ecumenical movement to reunite Christendom as a single Church has yet, despite its basic goodwill, to make much progress: the Churches have not even been able to agree on a single date for Easter, let alone to reconcile more fundamental issues. The divisions among the Christian Churches are in fact profound and could only be overcome by compromises that none is likely to accept. Let us take a look at the nature of the differences among the three major faiths and why they persist today from the Orthodox point of view.

Non-hierarchical, Orthodoxy recognises the authority of no single bishop over any other. To the Orthodox, the Pope is also a bishop – the Bishop of Rome – no less and no more. Because of the historical importance of his diocese, Rome, he would enjoy a very special rank as 'first among equals' – the first *in honour* among all bishops and patriarchs – were he not considered heretical by the Eastern Church. In Orthodox eyes, the Pope has exceeded his authority and misused his office, taking decisions upon himself that can only be made by the *oecumene* – the community of Christians – and has for this and other reasons excluded himself from that community. That his *ex cathedra* decisions might be infallible is thus unthinkable to the Orthodox.

Unlike the Protestants but like the Catholics, the Orthodox have seven sacraments: baptism, chrismation, marriage, ordination, confession, communion, and unction. The nature and purposes of some of these sacraments differ, however, between the Catholics and the Orthodox: confession and unction come particularly to mind. The Protestants have only two sacraments: baptism and communion – historically, the earliest ones.

The Orthodox reject two doctrines that are essential to Catholicism: purgatory and the immaculate conception of the Virgin Mary (the doctrine that Mary was freed of original sin immediately upon being conceived by her parents).

Readings from Holy Scripture are an important part of all Orthodox services. The living spirit of Orthodox Christianity is not to be found in the Gospel alone, however, but also in the sacraments, the Seven Councils, tradition, liturgical texts, hymns and other writings. After all, during the first, second, third and even parts of the fourth centuries of Christianity, before the New Testament was confirmed in its final form, thousands of true and great Christians, among them many saints, died without any knowledge of the Bible in general or the New Testament in particular. Thus, in Orthodoxy, knowledge of Holy Scripture is only one of several pillars of faith, whereas particularly in many Protestant Churches it might be termed the main pillar of faith.

Priests of the Orthodox Church may be married, as may ministers among the Protestants, though Orthodox priests, unlike Protestant ministers, must marry before they are ordained and may marry only once. Catholic priests may not marry at all. Neither the Orthodox nor the Catholic Church ordains female clergy, yet the Protestant churches do. In Orthodoxy, monks do not belong to particular 'orders' as Catholic monks do: they conform to the rules of their home monastery.

The Orthodox and Catholics stress ritual as a legitimate vehicle for the communication of the *Logos*, God's word; the Protestants stress the spoken word and intellectual message: the sermon. Orthodox cross themselves from right to left, Catholics from left to right, Protestants not at all. The Orthodox use leavened bread in the Eucharist as symbolic of the presence of the Holy Spirit; the

Catholics use unleavened bread. In Orthodoxy, Easter is calculated on the basis of the Julian calendar; in the Western Churches it is based on the Gregorian calendar. Orthodox clergy – priests and monks – are always bearded, whereas Catholic priests and Protestant clergy may be clean-shaven. Unlike Catholic and Protestant clergy, Orthodox priests and monks are always clothed in long robes quite distinct from modern dress.

Art and music have developed very differently in the Eastern and Western Churches. There is no sculpture in Orthodox churches, as there may be in both Catholic and Protestant ones, nor is there any three-dimensional artwork. The two-dimensional icons are considered the only appropriate visual medium for Orthodox worship. In Orthodox services, the human voice is the only musical instrument permitted, and in some Churches, such as the Greek Orthodox, even polyphonic chanting is not allowed.

These are just a few of the differences, and none of them is arbitrary: each Church has compelling arguments for its beliefs and practices.

For the Orthodox, the really insuperable obstacles to union with the other Christian Churches are, in the view of this author, the steeply hierarchical structure of the Catholic Church, capped by the papacy, and the exclusion of all but two sacraments among the Protestants. It is safe to say that the Orthodox would never recognise papal supremacy, as this contradicts the Orthodox view of the workings of the Holy Spirit, who descended originally upon not one but many persons. Nor would the Orthodox be willing to relinquish five essential sacraments and confine themselves exclusively to baptism and communion as the Protestants do.

There is also the crucial theological point of the *filioque* ('and the son' in Latin). By using the *filioque*, Western Christians take the position that, within the Trinity which forms the godhead, the Holy Spirit proceeds from both the Father and the Son. The Orthodox view God the Father as the sole source of the Holy Spirit, his role being generally that of Author and Father. They feel that the *filioque* makes the Holy Spirit lesser in might than the Father and the Son. This difference – highly technical as it may appear to some today – nevertheless affects the balance within the Trinity of Father, Son and Holy Spirit and is therefore pivotal within Christian theology. Orthodox furthermore point to the Gospel according to St John 15: 26, in which Christ says, 'when the Comforter is come, whom I will send unto you from the Father, even the Spirit of truth, which proceedeth from the Father, he shall testify of me.'

Another difference that is hard to pin down, but well worth mentioning nonetheless, is that Orthodoxy, unlike the Western Churches, generally steers clear of analysis and disputation about God.

Orthodoxy avoids positive statements about the nature of God as likely to be misleading due to the inevitable limitations of the human viewpoint and sticks to apophaticism: statements solely about what God is not.

Must there in fact be unity among the Churches? The energy expended on attempts toward unification might be better turned to the exercise of the great Christian precept of Love, that sure fount of tolerance, kindness and understanding among all humankind.

The Orthodox love their Church beyond disputation as it is and always has been, that is, as defined and confirmed by the Seven Ecumenical Councils during the first eight hundred years of our era. They love its elaborate, stately and undeviating ritual, rich in symbolism and significance; its other-worldly icons expressing their profound message in human faces; its ranks of familiar, sympathetic and ever-present saints; its embassy of all-encompassing love, both human and divine; and its essential egalitarianism. They look to their local bishop, priests, monks and nuns for understanding and guidance. They embrace the holiness of the seven sacraments and proclaim their belief through the Creed in its original form.

At the same time, the Orthodox Church leaves judgement to God: it certainly does not despise the other confessions or regard them with hostility. It honours their leaders and respects their adherents.

In this spirit, it welcomes you – whatever your beliefs – to visit its churches and services and to worship God. The fragrant incense, the chanting of the priests and cantors, the poetry of the psalms, the splendid vestments of the clergy, the majesty of the services, the beauty of the candlelight and icons, the marble, gold and silver and the brilliantly conceived Church structure itself all constitute an effort to glorify God as well as humanly possible. You are welcome to participate in this attempt.

⊙ *Abbot, cantor and priest at a country chapel consecration*

Easter Dates

In both East and West, Easter is the first Sunday after the first full moon after the vernal equinox, that day in spring in which day and night are equally long. According to the Gregorian calendar generally used throughout the world, the vernal equinox is 21 March, but according to the Julian calendar, it is 3 April.

The Greek Orthodox Church generally accepts the Gregorian calendar, so that it celebrates Christmas, for instance, on 25 December as in the West. The Orthodox Churches of Jerusalem, Russia and Serbia and the monasteries of Mount Athos, however, have stayed with the Julian calendar. In their desire to preserve Orthodox unity for Easter, the feast of feasts, all Orthodox Churches accept the calculation based on the Julian calendar, now thirteen days behind the Gregorian.

ORTHODOX AND WESTERN EASTER TO 2030

Year	Eastern Churches	Both East and West	Western Churches
2009	April 19		April 12
2010		4 April	
2011		24 April	
2012	April 15		April 8
2013	May 5		March 31
2014		20 April	
2015	April 12		April 5
2016	May 1		March 27
2017		16 April	
2018	April 8		April 1
2019	April 28		April 21
2020	April 19		April 12
2021	May 2		April 4
2022	April 24		April 17
2023	April 16		April 9
2024	May 5		March 31
2025		20 April	
2026	April 12		April 5
2027	May 2		March 28
2028		16 April	
2029	April 8		April 1
2030	April 28		April 21

Dates according to the Greek Orthodox Archdiocese of Australia

The Twelve Great Feasts and Easter

Orthodox (and Western) designation	Date	Event commemorated
Annunciation	25 March	The angel Gabriel announces to the Virgin Mary that she has been chosen to bear God's son.
Christmas	25 Dec	The birth of Jesus
Presentation	2 Feb	Christ is presented in the temple 40 days after his birth.
Theophany (Epiphany)	6 Jan	The adult Christ is baptised by St John
Transfiguration	6 Aug	Christ reveals himself in his divine glory to SS Peter, James and John on Mt Tabor.
Elevation of Holy Cross	14 Sept	Reverence of the holy cross upon which Christ was crucified.
Nativity of Theotokos	8 Sept	The birth of the Virgin Mary, Mother of God.
Theotokos Presentation	21 Nov	Mary is presented in the temple as a young girl.
Dormition of the Virgin	15 Aug	Mary 'falls asleep' in the Lord.
EASTER	Moveable: April/ May	Jesus Christ is resurrected from the dead.
Palm Sunday	1 week before Easter	Jesus' entry into Jerusalem
Ascension	40 days after Easter	Jesus' ascension into heaven
Pentecost	50 days after Easter	The Holy Spirit descends on Jesus' followers: the founding of the Orthodox Church

Index